Healing Environment

The Conscious Creation of

Health

Angela Levesque

All rights reserved. No part of the book may be used or reproduced in any manner whatsoever without written permission except in the case of brief quotations embodied in critical articles or reviews.

Copyright ©2013 by Angela Levesque
Hestia Health LLC
www.hestiahealth.com

Cover by Scott Truitt
Truitt Brand Design

Jacket Photo by Jan Schmidt
tomatobaby lifestyle photograph

Printed in the United States of America

ISBN-13: 978-0991066681

For my Grandma for giving me the inspiration and to Isaac and Shawn for supporting the journey.

Disclaimer

The information presented in the book is for informational purposes only and is not to be construed as medical advice. Please contact your health care provider before making any changes to your health program. While I am a firm believer that everyone needs to be a partner in their health care and that the self-care techniques outlined in this book are very valuable, they should be done in conjunction with your health care professional.

Table of Contents

Preface

Introduction … 1

Part I The Long Road Whole: The Global View

1. Are We Whole? … 7
2. Stress: A Culture of Imbalance … 16
3. Cultivating the Sustainable Self … 24
4. Our Health, Our Earth: Three Converging Emergencies … 34

Part II Moving From the Inside Out

5. Stress, Perception & the Body … 46
6. Holistic Fitness: Being Mindful Through Movement … 60
7. Food as Medicine, Whole Foods & the Holistic Perspective … 79
8. Our Toxic Burden: What Can We Control? … 90

Part III Calm Mind, Calm Body

9. The Mind/Body Relationship … 101
10. The Wellness Identity … 114
11. Gratitude and Transformation … 125
12. Relaxation and Beyond … 133

| 13 | Meditation for Conscious Healing | 142 |

Part IV Transcending Our Limits

14	Use the Force: Understanding Consciousness	155
15	The Energy Matrix: Healing the Spirit Within	166
16	Where Spirit Meets Science: Our New Focus	175

| Appendix | 183 |
| Notes | 197 |

Preface

My conscious spiritual journey began when I was 14, though I know the choices made of the lessons I would learn happened before my birth. It was then that my first grandparent passed away. As expected, I was deeply upset, but not because of his death, rather that he lived so long….suffering. In all of the memories I had of my grandfather, he had always been sick. Growing up in a religious environment, I had been taught of God's mercy, but I could see no mercy here, only the slow decline of a man I loved with all of my heart. This made me angry with God. Why was my Grandfather not shown the compassion that he deserved? Even then, watching the reaction of my family to his passing confused me. To me his death was the end of his suffering and the beginning of his life with God. Wasn't there relief in that? Surely people who had such a strong belief in the afterlife could see the blessings in this event. Maybe the afterlife didn't exist?

These were big questions for my 14-year-old brain to comprehend and they were a catalyst for my spiritual journey. In truth, even before this incident I always had many questions about God. The answer to all my inquiries was always the same, "Because it is in the Bible". That answer placated me for some time, but after my Grandfather passed I needed more answers. So I set out to find the answers I was looking for, beginning with a look at different religions. At that time I couldn't conceive of a relationship with God outside of religion, as I had no idea of spirituality outside of a religious context. I read books about Buddhism, Taoism and Zen philosophy. I experienced profound growth from reading those books - their teachings appealed to me intellectually, but also spiritually. There was no mention of war, rape and violence, like in the Old Testament, only enlightening concepts.

Consequently, I started meditating when I was 17. (I used to meditate in my closet, so my parents would remain unaware of my practice.) I remember the stillness used to scare me; that feeling of lightness and the awareness that my spiritual self wanted to be free of my physical body. This frightened me; for some part of me felt that I was doing something wrong against God. After moving away from home when I was 18, I started getting into the 'Beat' authors, shifting my focus from God, to Agnosticism to Nihilism. In many ways, I have spent my whole life looking for truth. At 20, I read Conversations with God by Neil Donald Walsch for the first time and it transformed me. It was then that I realized that our personal health and healing could not be separate from our spiritual growth. This is what we were missing; our health cannot exist outside of spirituality…outside of God.

It wasn't so much that I read that book and it presented new ideas, but that someone so easily and eloquently took my personal understanding of existence and put it on paper. It was confirmation to me that this life was about more than the accumulation of material wealth and goods - that there was more meaning to life than what was being sold to us. That book lit a fire within me that hasn't gone out.

I actually spent a good part of my late teens and early twenties experimenting with hallucinogenic drugs. Partly because I was filled with reckless abandon, living in a world where I didn't feel understood, and partly because I was looking for a truth that I knew existed, but couldn't grasp. Nobody else my age seemed to be filled with questions about the meaning of existence. Most of my experimentation was to find a quick and easy way to experience God. I knew that this thinly veiled world held many truths and I was hungry for them. Now, I know those truths will never be revealed through artificial means, but hey it was worth a shot. I never bought into the white picket fence ideal, or the American Dream. It never felt right and it was as artificial to me as the LSD I was taking as a means to be closer to God. I believe that many other people do not buy into the American Dream, consciously or unconsciously, and by trying to attain it, we are making ourselves ill. We are spiritual beings living a material existence and I don't believe this is what we were meant for, at least not anymore.

I came to the realization, in my early twenties, that if I really believed in the mind/body/spirit connection that I would have to learn about all aspects of self. I started yoga and continued with meditation to develop my connection to Spirit and became a veracious reader on spirituality, science and anything that could combine the two. There is the expression, "A jack of all trades, but a master of none". I really felt that this was what I was and for a long time, I saw this as a negative. I was gaining a level of knowledge of one topic and then moving on to the next. Now in my thirties, I see this more as one of my gifts. I have a wide view of many topics that relate to the issue of healing, not just the physical self, but all aspects that make us human. I know the world needs people to look at things in great detail, but we also need people who can see the larger puzzle while still grasping all the pieces and I hope that I am one of those.

As we stand here now, I see a world in crisis. We are seeing the same boom in industrialization and urbanization that we went through two hundred years ago in China and India. As I write this, our population is seven billion people and growing exponentially. Our world will not sustain the same kind and level of growth that brought us here. We are engaging in an unconscious feeding of the mechanisms that are consuming our resources at an alarming rate. It is time to bring these truths into our awareness and make better choices. These choices are integral to our health crisis; nothing exists in a vacuum. My hope for this book is that it will start the dialogue to better health and more importantly, a better world.

Introduction

Right now we are at the precipice of expanded human consciousness. There is an undercurrent, a force pushing us forward, but our minds and our self-imposed limitations are holding us back. We have over identified with our physical bodies, and without a true connection and appreciation for how the mind and spirit interact with the physical form, we have grown stagnant. This is the stem of our disease. Here in the West, we are suffering from diseases of lifestyle - diseases of choice. Some of these choices we made as individuals, and some of them were made for us by the external world that we all had a hand in creating. It is time to grow our awareness and extend it beyond our world of matter, but we can't do that until our bodies are up to the challenge. This requires us to create the optimal healing environment in the body and in doing this, we can change the world.

Our Health as a Catalyst

Everywhere you look you can see suffering. It is not a condition reserved for the poor or the meek - it is our spirit being unfulfilled. We are seeing more and more people suffering chronic illness, obesity, depression and anxiety and yet, we have charted this course unknowingly and unconsciously. We have drifted aimlessly in a world that asks individuals not to be accountable. It promotes hopelessness and helplessness and worst of all, complacency. The actions behind these thoughts have led us to apathy and poor health. But this is only one part of it. Humanity is currently undergoing a huge shift – an expansion of our consciousness. Our over identification with this third dimensional world has disallowed this knowing. As we resist this momentum, we also see a breakdown in our health. So if we create health, not just the mere absence of disease, but real health - we create a better world by allowing our consciousness the space to grow. The power then, lies within each one of us.

The Macrocosm to the Microcosm

This book looks at the large to the small. One can deny our entanglement with the infinitesimal and the universal, but in that exchange lies the answer to our health and the healing of the planet. The optimal healing environment is about creating stability in the body, but is achieved only when we find joy, peace and purpose. Purpose needs to be a thread interwoven in every aspect of our lives - from the profound to the most trivial of moments. While you may think that joy and purpose are more emotional states or concerns, they have a vibrational frequency and their own basis in our physiology. This connection must be forged on every level from the cell to the cosmos. We can use our health as a catalyst to alter the lager human condition, which right now is suffering. Our current health crisis is a manifestation of larger societal, cultural and environmental issues and a suppression of Spirit.

The Optimal Healing Environment

I am going to refer to the optimal healing environment throughout the book. Basically, it is about creating a stable, resilient physiology in the body, which can only truly be done when we utilize, understand and engage in all dimensions of our wellness. It is in this framework that expanded consciousness has the ability to thrive.

There are 5 components to creating the optimal healing environment. Each component will be interwoven throughout the book.

1. We need to move our bodies in creative movement every day. Our bodies were designed to move and they must do so every single day. This can be as simple as a walk in nature.

2. We need to manage/mitigate and eliminate stressors in our life. This is not only about taking time out to relax, but also by challenging the very way we create our lives. We are creators, not victims. In taking the time to go within, we can find what things we can do without.

3. We need to eat considering food as our medicine. Nothing impacts our health more than what we put in our bodies. This means we need to be eating real, nutrient rich, whole foods. This also requires us, as a collective, to challenge our methods of food production and the toxins we put into our environment.

4. We need to become right thinkers and conscious healers while becoming aware of the messages we are sending to our bodies via our thoughts. Our incessant self-talk and

self-imposed limitations from the egoic mind, hinders our healing potential.

5. We need to understand the energetic/spiritual nature of our beings and use this knowledge for our self-healing. The world is vibration and when we can engage and intuit the frequencies, we can unlock our limitless potential.

The optimal healing environment can change things for us individually and globally because the bi-products of achieving this state have an impact on the whole. It develops our awareness on every level. It helps us to understand the impact that our choices have on the energetic matrix of the planet. It helps us to move beyond our ego mind and our fear based choices so we are able to challenge the systems that no longer serve us. It cultivates self-love, which leads to better decision-making and reiterates our connection to one another. It will allow us to better get in touch with our intuition and creativity so we can solve the problems that lie before us. To put it another way, it leads to a physiology that is conducive to raising our consciousness, individually and globally.

How to Use This Book

The first section takes a global view of healing and the issues that are contributing to our poor health. It helps us to understand the impact that our individual choices have on the larger environment. It asks you to challenge the rituals, routines and systems that are in place. Because until we look at the way the systems are set-up, the policies that are being made and industries that perpetuate the status quo, we won't appreciate how systemic the problem is. Once we frame the conversation, we can look within and challenge our own views of health and healing.

HEALING ENVIRONMENT

The second and third section focus on the body and mind. This part of the book gives us hope. Using the body and our health as a catalyst, it gives well-researched self-care techniques that can be useful in dealing with chronic illness. I know that as individuals if we create health in our own bodies and our own systems, we can create the change we need in the world to live sustainable, joyful lives. The health I am speaking about is not through drugs, but through personal growth and awareness. The final section explores the nature of consciousness, energy medicine and also contains a new paradigm for our world, for I know that our health and our spirituality are inextricably linked. I truly believe that the same things that are going to heal our bodies are the same things that will heal the world. So join me in improving your health and help heal the world one body at a time.

Part I

The Long Road Whole:

The Global View

Chapter 1
Are We Whole?

Disease is resistance. Resistance comes in many forms and it can manifest in our thoughts, our feelings, and in our bodies. There is resistance to different/better choices, resistance to learning and growth, resistance to flow and resistance to listening to our innermost self. We live in a time and place in civilization that it is almost impossible to hear our own thoughts, let alone be in tune with our own spirit. The external stimuli and internal congestion overwhelms our systems and little by little we begin to breakdown. This breakdown can occur mentally, emotionally and spiritually until our bodies follow suit to a point that it can no longer be ignored. Why do we do this and where has this lack of connection from our bodies, minds and environment taken us? Where has this disconnection from each other taken us?

What does it mean to be whole? Can whole exist completely within the self or will there always be a component of unity or oneness required? What does the word healing really mean? These are questions that need to be asked and answered, not just by the leaders of the world, but by each one of us individually. We need to look on a systems level, on a global scale and in a universal context. To heal and to become whole are one in the same. Before you move on, take a moment and breathe that idea in, that wholeness and healing are one and the same. The holistic perspective isn't just the latest buzzword; it actually means something profound. We are coming from a place where each one of us is seen as a whole person, not just a system or a symptom or an illness, but a whole person in its entirety.[1] Very often we use the words healing and curing synonymously, but they are truly different creatures. Healing is wholeness. A person with terminal cancer can be healed in his last days, but not cured. As Dr. Andrew Weil explains, "It is possible to have an inner sense of wholeness, perfection, balance and peace even if the physical body is not perfect"[2]. This will not happen if we only identify with our physical selves.

The truth is more than that, as individuals we are a complete whole, but we are also a holograph, a complete representation of a larger system - a global system, a spiritual matrix. Just as one system can change the whole, one individual can affect the world. This is the essence of consciousness. This way of looking at our health, using it as a catalyst for change, gives us the opportunity and the possibility to change the way we do healthcare and the way in which we engage in the world. In fact, that change has already begun.

If we look at this, I mean really regard the holistic perspective with merit, how does it change the way we look at our health and most importantly our healing? The mind/body/spirit connection is another term that is thrown around, but it is a very hard concept to pin point.

Perhaps, it is too expansive in nature - something too intangible to grasp. Yet, it is that connection that is the key to our health and the healing of our planet. There is no way to become whole, that is to say heal, without understanding that connection, and thusly the flow of information or intelligence that exists among its parts.

Yoga is an amazing example of the integration of mind/body/sprit, but it has become a crutch in society. "Oh we do yoga, we get it." But the truth is that if we are really going to raise our consciousness, change our health, the planet, and ourselves we need to understand why yoga is so transforming. I think my biggest issue with yoga becoming mainstream here in the West, is that it is touted as an enabler of this connection; however most of the popular forms of yoga here are so far removed from its origin. Yoga as we know it is only one limb, in the 8 limbs in yoga, called Asana. The 8 limbs of yoga is a way of living with the true integration of spirituality in everyday life. Yoga is a guideline for spiritual living. It is a complete system of health and wholeness. We have ejected out the parts of yoga that really allows us to experience the spirit and to understand it; to know what it is to be mindful, to have awareness of the body as it moves through the spiritual matrix. So, in the West we are still left with a lofty ideal of the mind/body/sprit with no real awareness of how that plays out in everyday life and even less of an understanding how to integrate it into our health care system. This is the crux of the problem and the stem of our poor health, but if we use our health as the jumping off point and allow it to lead us to greater spiritual discoveries imperative to the human condition, we create change from the inside out.

The Eight Limbs of Yoga[3]

The Yoga Sutras is an eight-fold path that offers guidelines for living a spiritual life.

Yama: Universal morality - This includes such things as your ethics and integrity.

Niyama: Spiritual observances - This includes your own personal practice such as attending church and practicing meditation.

Asanas: Body postures - This is what we are most familiar with here in the West, looks at our bodies as a temple of discipline and concentration.

Pranayama: This is the practice of breath control and the movement of Prana or life force moving through the body with breathing exercises.

Pratyahara: Withdrawals - This is the detachment from the outside world and a journey inward. This allows us to become aware of our habits and limiting behaviors.

Dharana: Concentration - This is the preparation for meditation, learning to concentrate on a single point.

Dhyana: Meditation or Contemplation - This is the stilling of the mind, transcending thought.

Samadhi: Union with the Divine - This is the point of transcendence or merging into oneness.

The Spirit Within

What happened to the spirit in us? We keep talking about the mind/body/spirit, but where is the Spirit? Every major religion has a word, or multiple words for it, and yet it remains elusive to us. Why is it that we have no awareness of what holds us together as an individual, a society, as a nation and as a universe? Why do many of us not even acknowledge its existence? The answer is that we are disconnected. The Spirit has been devalued, downplayed and even distorted, but in our hearts we know there is something more. As humans we spend a portion of our time debating religion, resources, land, wars, rights, but where is the time and opportunity to engage and experience the Spirit and intelligence that binds us. Connects us. Our education systems, our health care, our governments do not give us the tools that allow us to experience our wholeness. It remains an intellectual conversation that is rooted in our physical, material reality. These conversations are of mute point once we understand the connectedness, not through linear, reductionist means, but through spiritual transformation. The way to Spirit is not through our minds, but in each breath and in each heart. That is where we create union. It is through meditation, mindfulness and stillness that we experience the true nature of reality and the source of our healing.

In Christianity, the Holy Spirit is the least understood part of the Holy Trinity, just as it is with the spirit in the mind/body/spirit trinity, but it is what is necessary to make us whole and for us to heal ourselves personally and globally. It is always so interesting to me that we mirror one another on various levels of existence. For example, why are we so scared to die? There are very few among us that aren't afraid of death, yet aren't many of us promised an afterlife? We fear death because we have not understood life. We are too entangled in the physical realm to truly understand the energetic and spiritual aspects of the universe, so we have created drastic life saving measures in order to extend our lives, to put off the inevitable. It is an interesting dichotomy, because we cling to life while making choices that lead us to complicated, untimely deaths.

Mindfulness & Healing

What is necessary to understand and engage with the spirit side of the equation? Spirit resides in the moment of now, so the most important and necessary component is to be present. That is to say, to be mindful. According to Katherine Isaac of Massachusetts General[4], mindfulness requires attentive observation, critical curiosity, a Beginner's Mind and most importantly, presence. If we break down each of those we can really understand one of the major concepts of this book. Attentive observation will seem very counter intuitive in our multi tasking world. Multi tasking, in a sense, is the antithesis of mindfulness. In order to be present you must be observant and have your focus in the moment. Have you ever had the experience where you have been telling a story and you lose your train of thought? Most likely, you have allowed your mind to wander from the present thus causing you to forget what you were talking about. You weren't even paying attention to your own story. That example illustrates the complexity of the human mind, our ability to exist in many different spaces at once.

The second component Isaac talks about is critical curiosity, the desire to gain insight and to seek truth instead of being in a state of general passivity. It is to have a thirst to expand, inquire, and understand the underpinnings of a situation. Thirdly, she talks about going into things with a 'Beginner's Mind'. This term comes from the Zen Buddhist tradition, which means to come into an experience with an open and non-judgmental mind. Mindfulness is not about critical thinking; it is a state of allowing. I don't want there to be confusion about the terms allowing and passivity. In passivity there is disinterest and inactivity; in allowing there is intention to permit an experience. As Deepak Chopra illuminated for us in Ageless Body Timeless Mind, "Intention is the active partner of attention".[5] The last, and in my opinion, the most necessary component which allows all others to exist, is presence. You cannot be mindful if you are not in the present moment. Mindfulness is necessary to healing and it is also necessary to grasp our oneness with each other. It helps us to build awareness, calm the body, mitigate stress and negative thoughts. It is a critical concept that promotes the optimal healing environment.

Our Healing Capacity

Our bodies have an innate ability to heal, (we see this process all the time after we cut ourselves.) From a physical perspective, there are three distinct components that happen in healing: reaction, regeneration and adaptation.[6] These responses are innate and universal to all living organisms. However, this ability is not a mere physiological process; it is a spiritual, mental, emotional and energetic one as well. If there is a failure in any part of the system, we have the inability to heal. Stress is an example of this. Very often due to things outside of our control, whether environmental or genetic or even within our control - our systems become overwhelmed. When this happens the body loses its ability for self-healing; no system can work effectively when it has been overrun.

A few years back, I lived near a huge river in a large metropolitan area. The river looked heavily polluted to me and I was often disturbed when parents would let their children play in it. All up and down the river, heavy industry had settled along its banks. At one time, I had made mention to somebody that the river was very heavily polluted. He told me that it was relatively clean compared to the years before environmental restrictions were in place. I thought that the humans over the last decade or so had made efforts to clean up the river. The man laughed at me and said, "The river cleaned up the river; humans just needed to stop overwhelming her systems, and she was able to take care of the rest."

In nature everywhere, the same types of self-regulatory systems exist. In Biology, these systems with the ability to regulate and counteract the influences that would change the internal environment are called negative feedback loops. The negative in the title refers to the system's ability to balance out the error signal by returning the body back to a set point.[7] The body and the earth have a drive toward homeostasis and as long as the system does not become overwhelmed, these systems work very well. That is why balance is so important and why living mindfully is tantamount to our thriving as a population. All systems are interdependent and interconnected, for this reason, if one is misaligned others can follow suit. Conversely, sometimes you can approach one aspect of the system to bring balance to the disharmonious one.

This is what healing is, finding the balance between all aspects of ourselves and our environment. This requires a drastic departure from all that we currently hold dear. A focus on the external material reality will never bring us balance because we are focusing on the wrong things.

This is our resistance and this is our downfall, if we don't start to get it right. Our bodies and minds are paying a steep price for denying this truth. We are spiritual beings first and foremost. We must create a vessel that allows our spirit to flourish, not stagnate. Christina Baldwin wrote in the book Life's Companion: Journal Writing as a Spiritual Quest,

"I am not my body," she said. "I am not my work or role. I am not my gender. I am not my nationality. I am not a human being......I am a spiritual being having a human experience."[8]

It is that awareness that will bring us back to our set point, to our new beginning.

Chapter 2
Stress: A Culture of Imbalance

Stress in another word we use so often that it almost has lost its meaning. "I am stressed out." It has become such an accepted part of life, yet in our society we make no effort to change this. We all just accept it as the status quo and move on. The trouble with that is that stress plays a major role in our health. In fact, 60-90% of all doctor's visits are related to stress.[1] It is either the root cause or an exacerbating factor in almost every illness that plagues our society. And furthermore, there is no greater example of the holistic perspective than we see with stress. Though the example is a negative one, stress shows how one aspect of ourselves directly affects others. When someone is under stress, it can manifest itself physically, through hormone release, headaches or gastrointestinal upset. It can manifest itself psychologically, through anxiety and depression. It can manifest itself mentally, by decreasing our concentration or creative abilities. The symptoms go on and on, but it impacts all aspects of who we are. In order to truly deal with our health, we need to mange or eliminate our stressors, but even more than that we need to challenge what we accept as acceptable.

Challenging the System

In order to accomplish this, it may require a complete overhaul in how we operate our lives, in our homes and in the workplace. Elizabeth Gilbert in her book, Eat Pray Love, talks very eloquently about how Americans love entertainment, but do not know what pleasure is. She remarks, "Americans don't really know how to do nothing".[2] Consequently, we lose out on finding joy or pleasure in the little things, so we do them unconsciously or outsource them for the sake of convenience. We are unable to enjoy simplicity. There is a weird sense of accomplishment and praise from others if we are so busy that we don't have a moment to relax. I had a woman in one of my classes on stress reduction who exemplified this perfectly. I always give my participants homework, such as stress reduction techniques, so they continue to engage in the learning and changing of habits over the week. She came to the first couple classes and would always complain that she didn't have time to do the homework; her life was just too crazy to fit it in. It is funny she couldn't make any connections between why she needed the stress reduction class and how her life was set up. She became a victim of her circumstance, but never even questioned for a second that it could be different. That is our problem globally as well.

Stress reduction techniques do more than just relax the body - they build awareness. Humans are sorely lacking awareness of self or situation. Awareness is what is going to change us, but we can't choose differently if we don't know any better. Through awareness we can take deliberate action, make conscious choices and no longer be a prisoner to habits and the workings of the egoic mind. This only happens if we take time out from the daily rat race and spend some time in solitude. This is why we are so stressed. It is a vicious cycle. We are stressed because we build our lives to be hectic and then we spend little time being connected and this creates more stress. Then we create busy, to take our minds off of our stress. It is hard for people to be able to sit in their stuff. To really let what they feel or experience to sit with them, to let it be their companion. We don't like to be uncomfortable, but it is in these moments that we can become aware. Until we stand on the edge of comfort, we can never grow.

Time to Unplug

I think that we need to spend a portion of each day unplugged. No phones, no Internet, no television and maybe even no talking. We can't know what we are missing out on until we allow it space to manifest. I would even go so far as to suggest we reinstitute the Sabbath as well as daily time outs. Even if you are not religious, does it not seem like a good idea to take a day off once a week? No cell phones, mobile devices, Internet - only friends, family and food. Doesn't that sound heavenly? I remember as a kid we had a municipal vote over whether or not to allow shopping on Sundays. I was only twelve at the time, but I remember the outrage over the possibility of allowing stores to be open on a Sunday. A mere twenty years later and it would be equally outrageous to consider the stores not open. Now we are open every Sunday, every holiday and all for the sake of making more money. Even if you are not religious, could you not benefit from some time off to spend with people you love - having conscious, mindful interactions? I believe spiritual currency is worth more than the almighty dollar on any day of the week.

I have recently met a woman who is an Ordained Buddhist Chaplain, and as part of her commitment to that service she is required to spend two months out of the year in silence. When she first told me that, my heart ached. It sounded so beautiful and honest. Every week she spends half a day in silence and then does several eight-day silent retreats. I can't imagine the things she learns about herself and about the greater truths of humanity and existence. Could we change the world if we all made the same commitment to ourselves?

We are more connected electronically than ever before, but it is not that connection that really counts. It moves us away from a place of awareness, again of the situation and ourselves. I often see groups of teenagers hanging out together and all of them are on their phones communicating with other people. These are not real exchanges that grow the heart and nourish the soul. Not only that, but we are butchering the English language with the texting lingo. At least on some level we were able to get our ideas across with language and now we are dismantling that too for the sake of convenience. This isn't a problem that has only started with this recent generation of young folks. We are their teachers.

As parents, we have created hectic schedules and allowed the constant bombardment of information and input to manifest an illusion that busy equals good and it is necessary for us to make it in this world. The opposite is true and now we have pulled our children into the insanity. We give them homework every night in elementary school and enroll them in soccer, baseball, guitar and Spanish classes. Now, not only is our work life hectic, the after school schedule is a pressure cooker. Now there is no time for a meal together. Why not get fast food? The number one consumers of fast food are middle-income families.[3] And so the spiral starts; a downward spiral of stress, exacerbated by poor nutrition, inadequate rest and less and less mindful, social connection. These are the very things that make us ill and guess what? They are making us ill.

The Spirit of a Meal

So often we forget the importance of breaking bread. There is spirit in a meal. It gives us energy in a very literal sense, but it also feeds our mind/bodies and souls. We have forgotten the importance it has in our lives to bless our families, fuel our movement and provide opportunities for creativity to flow. We see our food as something that simply sustains life instead of that which births it. Food is our medicine and it is the single most important factor in the health of our bodies. Our food provides us with the foundation from which all other life processes arise.

I think that it is even more than that. As a child, I remember nothing more comforting than being with my family eating a meal. A meal that was cooked at home with whole ingredients, made with love and with my well being in mind. As we sat there eating, we did much more than just eat. We broke bread, we shared, we laughed and filled the room with the aromas of food, and also, love. There is healing in that, better than any drug. Food and family, that connection, is where we gain the strength for all other of life's opportunities. We miss out on the healing when we

> rush around, eating unconsciously in the car in between soccer and piano lessons. We miss out on the healing when we make a meal from a box without a thought to its meaning or lack of value. And we also miss out on the opportunity to share the value of this experience with our children. Each moment, we teach our children through our actions that which we value. These fundamentals of our existence, making a meal and eating it with your family, are too important to be discarded.
>
> We need to return to that place as a family, a community and as a world. Remember what it is to create a meal with purpose and intention for well-being. To sit mindfully with our families and share the food of our spirit and the nourishment of our undivided attention. Take the opportunity not just to hear one another, but to really listen….to connect. This is the Spirit of a meal.

There is an exciting new trend in medicine these days toward integrative medicine. I see this as an offshoot of our expanding consciousness globally. As humans we are requiring a system that matches our currently unconscious need for wholeness. This is the combination of conventional modern medicine with the addition of complementary and alternative therapies. The conventional medical establishment is coming to realize the importance of spirituality, energy medicine, stress reduction and nutritional and environmental factors - treating the person as a whole and not just its parts. The key to complementary medicine, which may be its greatest gift, but also its biggest default, is that it includes the individual in their health.

Today we are facing diseases of choice and we need to choose better. We can't wait until our health begins to fail and then go to the doctor for a quick fix. We can no longer hand over our health; we are part of the partnership. I like to compare our health to a car. We wait until the check engine light goes on, take the car into the mechanic, hand over the keys and say, "Call me when it is fixed". This mentality is not working for us – we need to be accountable. It is up to us to be educated, resourceful and aware. We do this by utilizing resources that are already out there, but mostly we do this by listening to our own inner wisdom. Our inner being, which can only be heard in stillness.

These illnesses or physical disruptions are messages and we need to decipher and interpret their meaning. We have unbelievable power to heal ourselves, each other and the earth. All we need to do is wake up and listen. It takes more for us to resist the call, than it does to allow it. This is offered to us through various complementary and alternative modalities. They are here to empower us, and the more integrative our system becomes, the better it is for our health and healthcare system.

This gets some people excited, even hopeful, but others still want the quick fix. There truly needs to be a partnership between our medical community and the individual. Between our communities and the individual. This isn't about Socialism or government control, but about the people and their communities - locally and globally. So, let us aim higher and dream bigger than some of us have ever imagined.

We need a different paradigm and we are the writers of that shift. We are the trailblazers who can dare to choose differently - deliberately. Our time is now and the world needs us to wake up and use our health as the catalyst to create a great human existence.

Chapter 3

Cultivating the Sustainable Self

Several years ago I went to see a talk about the New Economy at the Muse Studio in Boise, ID.[1] They had four local people come and talk about how they saw the new economy being built out of the ashes of the economic crisis. A woman from a local CSA (community supported agriculture) farm, talked about how the economy should be built strong from the ground up. That in order to create a viable and strong economic climate in the country, each individual city needs to create a strong local economy. Part of her vision was that individuals needed to get more involved in their food supply, whether that was growing what they could in their own personal garden or by getting involved with a CSA. Her point was that it is necessary to provide for the needs of the community locally, and this is not only a wise environmental option, but also it keeps the money in the area and furthers the goal of a viable local and global economy. Her third point was that we need to collaborate and build local networks so we can be a well-informed populace who are able to provide for each other's needs. This not only served the other two points, but it made it easy for the community to buy locally when they knew where to procure their goods and services. After thinking long and hard about those points, not only from an economical or an ecological standpoint, but from a health care standpoint, I came to realize that those perspectives would serve in our healing as well.

In both the economical and ecological models we need to manage resources. As humans, we also need to become expert personal resource managers. To do this we need to broaden our definition of resources. It is not just our time and money, but our hobbies, our skills, our communities, our health and our sense of purpose that keep us well. If we define stress as our perceived resources not meeting our perceived demands, than we need to consider both how we manage resources and how to allocate them properly.

Time and money do need to be considered, managed and allocated appropriately. This is important, but it all goes back to what makes us happy. Stuff will not bring us joy. This is a huge part of our problem and our current economic crisis. Managing and allocating our money would be easier if we found our joy first. Our joy is priceless and is found through purpose, connection and true self-acceptance.

In addition to managing money and time, we need to use stress reduction to manage our body's resources, that is to say our health. Our body's ability to resist and cope with stress is key to the internal healing environment. This means we need to use some methods of stress reduction.

We will be talking more about that in chapter 5. Our bodies need upkeep, and that is where cultivation comes in. We need to tend to and take deliberate care of our self. Prevention is so much easier than treatment after the fact. Shifting the way we see food, physical activity, and stress reduction as means of preventive medicine would go a long way in fixing our health care crisis. Our current health care system is broken. Disease care is not effective and it is expensive. Our focus needs to be prevention and to do this we need to bring in other practitioners from other perspectives that shine in the areas of prevention. E.g. Naturopathic Medicine, Ayurvedic Medicine and Holistic Nutrition to name a few. This should be a community endeavor of the entire health care community.

We Already Know What Matters

In the Blue Zones research, Dan Buettner looked at the areas around the earth that have the biggest concentrations of centenarians (people who live to be over 100). They found some similar results regardless of locale, income or race. People who have community support and connection, ate primarily plant-based diets, woke up with a sense of purpose, moved creatively and kept moving their whole lives - lived longer, happier lives.[2] Looking at some of these factors in depth we can see the parallels between what is necessary for our healing, but also the health of the earth. There is healing power in connection and community, there is healing power in purpose, and there is healing power in good food and creative movement. We will discuss the importance of a holistic diet and exercise in the next section. First, we need to look at our connection to each other.

The Healing Power of Connection

The number one killer right now in the United States is Cardiovascular Disease (CVD). For years our focus was just on diet and exercise, but it is more than that. Our hearts are sick from lack of connection, and lack of purpose. Dean Ornish says in his book, Love and Survival: 8 Pathways to Intimacy & Health, "Our survival depends on the healing power of love, intimacy and relationships. Physically. Emotionally. Spiritually. As individuals. As communities. As a country. As a culture. Perhaps even as a species."[3]

In fact, we have a great example of this in Roseto Pa, now known as the Roseto Effect. This community has been the source of study on the effect of group cohesion and community. Back in the mid fifties and sixties, a group of Italian American families settled in the Roseto, Pa area. This group of people consisted of many multigenerational families co-existing in a tight knit community. They were primarily blue-collar families where many smoked and drank and ate heavy Italian meals. Even though their lifestyle choices and diet would normally put them at risk for CVD, this community had half the rate of the rest of America during that time. It was only when the community began moving and separating, largely when the younger generations moved away for college for the first time, that the CVD rates returned to the values found in the rest of the country.[4]

We used to have those kinds of villages to raise our children in and we lost that, but just because our biological families may be far away, that doesn't mean we can't be part of a village. In fact, we must. Social connection has health benefits far deeper than what meets the eye. Jeanne Achterberg did some profound work at the University of Hawaii on how distance intentionality i.e. prayer, energy healing etc., from a healer affected the brain function of the recipient. In her study, published by the Journal of Complementary and Alternative Medicine, she matched eleven healers in bonded client relationships. They had the healer send distance intentionality in on and off increments to the recipient in a fMRI. She noticed significant results in brain activation between the send and no send groups.[5] Now this is just a preliminary study, but it requires our attention.

Connection is more than skin deep. In the Roseto example we saw that the sense of community had a protective effect. In the study by Jeanne Achterberg, we know that the bonded relationship can be felt even over a distance. Now think about your normal and natural reaction to your sick or hurt child. The first thing you do is pull them close. You hold them. There is healing occurring even beyond your touch and your soothing words. When we don't feel like we have to do it alone, we can deal with stressful situations better. Social support has been well-studied and we know that it can have a protective effect against stress.[6] It decreases our rates of depression and feelings of isolation. All of that leads us to make better choices and those choices ultimately affect our health.

We have seen the rise of social media under the guise that we can stay connected. But it is not connectedness that we are offered with this advancing technology. It gives us the ability to disengage from those in our immediate surroundings and the ability to perform multiple tasks at the same time, maybe even holding several conversations with multiple people. We do this with cell phones, iPads even iPods, anything to not be present. It is now completely socially acceptable to ignore the people right beside you. We are isolated, yet surrounded by many. We are splitting our attention several times over. Neither the immediate environment of the person, or the person on the other end of the line or text is receiving our full attention. This phenomenon has not been well studied, but preliminary research is showing that although we think that our multi tasking is putting us ahead, we are actually doing all the tasks sub-par.[7] My concern is less with the efficiency in the tasks, but what about connection?

How many aspects of our daily lives are driven by mindless pleasantries and small talk? I will admit that I am the worst small talker. I used to work in a coffee shop and I had to teach myself small talk from watching fellow employees. I am so awkward trying to spout pleasantries. Instead I would rather remain silent or discuss the meaning of existence, than talk about the weather. We allow ourselves to run off these programs that are the exact opposite of Deepak Chopra's idea of conscious living.[8] Conscious living is important for our health and the planet. We need to interact with people and establish connections. This can be as simple as a nod, a smile and a loving intention. A brief, real acknowledgment of person's existence is better than an artificial pleasantry. When all of the attachments are released and the illusions stripped, isn't that what people ache for - that someone really sees them with love, and respect?

Connection in Health Care

Think about how this would improve health care, if we engaged in mindful communications with our health care provider. The average doctor interrupts the patient after 23 seconds of speaking.[9] Is that an example of conscious living or is that the doctor running off a program as well? We can't put all the blame on the doctor - we need to fulfill our end of the bargain. In order to heal on a mind/body/spirit level we need to see our role in the partnership. We have a responsibility to be an active partner.

Let's create a view of this interaction that creates a mindful exchange between the doctor and the patient. What if the doctor comes in and the two take a few moments to take five deep breaths together? This puts their awareness into the present moment and it helps to attune the two individuals with each other. Attunement is to bring one another into a harmonious or responsive relationship.[10] Now they are actively engaged with each other mind, body and spirit. Think about how much more information that they would receive from one another. The physician and the patient would be able to communicate on multiple planes. Admittedly, at this moment in civilization, only a relative few people are "sensitive" enough to really appreciate the subtle shifts in vibration, but the more we tap into these energies, the easier it will become. After the breathing, they could begin their verbal communication while continuing to be mindful. Remember that one of the components of mindfulness is a Beginner's Mind. This would require the physician to really listen to the whole idea that the patient is presenting instead of making a snap judgment. There is healing to be done even before the treatment begins.

Having a loving heart and open ear creates a healing exchange between the two people.

The Healing in Purpose

Let's look at some those key factors that allow people to live long and disease free lives. Since this book aims to look at chronic illness as a reflection of more global truths, then let's look at how truths of health exist globally. Do you know what your purpose is? Do you wake up each day and know why you are on this planet? I don't think that most people can readily answer that question. For a long time, I don't think I could answer it with any certainty. I also think that our purpose shifts and changes as we grow and learn. It would be a mistake to get attached to your purpose. Maybe your purpose is to help your child grow into a loving and caring adult. What would happen when that child grows up? Your purpose can be dynamic, but it is still important to find meaning in your everyday life. That is what it means to have a purpose - to find meaning in our actions. This requires us to be conscious of our actions in the first place. I teach a class on mind/body weight loss and one of the take home messages is that we need to find our joy and happiness first before we can lose the weight in any enduring manner. We do this all the time. If only I was thin or rich or had a better job then I could be happy. We never think the answer is to find happy first, and then attempt the external wants.

We have seen from people who win the lottery that money does not bring happiness. If you were depressed before winning, a year later you will be depressed again.[11] A big part of finding joy and happiness is living our lives aligned with our purpose. There are many studies that show the effect that purpose has on our mental well-being, but now we are increasingly seeing studies where it impacts our physical well-being as well. Purpose has been shown to increase longevity, decrease our risk of Alzheimer's and pain sensations.[12] It turns out that wandering aimlessly through life leads to poor health behaviors and this all makes sense if you think about it. The more you feel that life has meaning and that you are living your life with purpose, the more likely you will be to find joy. People who are happy and joyful make better choices. When as a country, we are dying from poor choices, maybe this is something to consider.

Connection, purpose, mindfulness, skills and hobbies are all important to our health. Much like in ecology, we also need to develop these resources. I call this chapter "Cultivating the Sustainable Self" for a reason. We need to prepare, develop and improve ourselves in order to have enduring health. So many of us stop learning as we get older. This is one reason for our decline in mental health as we age. If we kept reading and learning our minds would stay sharper. One of the reasons I love teaching community education classes is that you get people who still want to learn about new things. The point of the class is not to make them an expert on a subject, but to introduce them to one. Also, people who volunteer generally have a more positive outlook on life. They are able to help others, provide a service and feel good about what they have done.[13] Consider volunteering if you suffer from an illness, it will change your mindset, get you active and give you a sense of community and purpose. All of these things keep us healthy. All of these things matter on a larger scale.

10 Ways to Cultivate the Sustainable Self

1. Learn to relax, spend more time in recreational pursuits

2. Eat more plant based foods

3. Make a list of all your resources both personal and in the community and allocate them appropriately based on what brings you the most joy

4. Move your body creatively

5. Hug someone everyday

6. Volunteer

7. Take a class

8. Read a new book every month

9. Eat your food at the table with people you love

10. Spend time in mindful solitude

Chapter 4

Our Health, Our Earth:

Three Converging Emergencies

Our planet is in crisis just as we are. Bente Hansen says in her book, The New World of Self Healing, "All that we see happening in our natural environment is mirroring what is happening within the individuals on our planet."[1] There is hope for us if we can just live in harmony with our earth. People like to argue that it is conceited of humans to think we could have an effect on the earth and the environment. They like to argue over the science of climate change and/or global warming, but I think we can have this discussion without talking about that. All we need is a little common sense and the want to see what is happening outside of this political debate.

Food Supply & Production

We are under the illusion that our food supply is infinite. It is not, and we will need a place to grow our food. The more we pollute, the worse it is for the environment, and the worse it is for our bodies. There are several things that need to change immediately in order to change our health. The fast food industry as we know it, needs to be eliminated. The food wreaks havoc on our systems and destroys the environment.[2] It has been the single biggest factor in changing our food production and delivery systems. As China becomes more accustomed to our Westernized diet, the fast food industry is growing at a phenomenal pace. Our world will not support that growth. In fact, the company president for McDonald's Asia said back in July 2011, "We're now opening a restaurant every other day".[3] Think about the environmental impact of this and this is but one restaurant chain. Genetically modified food is not the answer. The energetic imprint of the food is false and our bodies know it. The plants know it. The bees know it. We cannot look towards GMOs to solve our food production woes.

How we grow our food must change. We need to go back to small scale, preferably, organic farms that support our regional growth. Factory farms wreak havoc on our environment, causing pollution, depletion of topsoil and decreases necessary biodiversity. We are being sold a lie that small farms cannot support the population. That is true if what we want to eat comes from a drive through window. This shift I am speaking of includes the way we feed our bodies. In the new paradigm, there is no room for high calorie, nutrient poor food, comprised mostly of corn and soybeans. It won't work for the environment and it is not working for our bodies. We are already beginning to see a shift in the marketplace. The organic sector is making huge gains, but it must be accompanied by a shift in consciousness. We cannot just ban what we don't want or like as that leads to further resistance. This change has to occur within, first. When the environment is bio diverse, when there is respect for the topsoil, and the ground water; food production can be much higher than that produced by a factory farm. Factory farms require so much infusion of herbicides and pesticides because the monocultures allow weeds and bugs to monopolize, creating a vicious cycle.[4] Another concern is desertification or the loss of productive farmland into wasteland. This happens through our mismanagement of the land and misuse of resources. When we remove much of the vegetation it allows the land to fall prey to both wind and water erosion. We are seeing this occur on a large scale in both Asia and Africa.[5] Remember those two continents contain a large majority of the earth's population.

    We need to get over our lust for cheap food and cheap clothing. Our want for cheap products changes the global marketplace. For example, the way in which we subsidize our food makes it cheaper for third world nations to purchase our crops than grow their own. This is detrimental to their already devastated economies. The subsidies have another impact as well. The subsidies for corn, sugar and soy allow food to be cheap, but it is this food that makes us fat and unhealthy.[6] I commend the current administration wanting to deal with childhood obesity, but unless they look at their subsidies and how that is directly related to the obesity problem, then it is just lip service. We need to eat what our local environment provides for. We need to eat food from farms and not from boxes. Shipping food across a continent not only requires huge energy inputs, but also requires that the food contain mass amount of preservatives. It would be far more nutritious for our bodies, if it did not have to remain mold and spoil free for unnatural amounts of time. When food is picked green, it does not even come close to having all the would be nutrients if it were allowed to ripen in the ground. This is also an increasing problem in the organic sector as large multinationals edge into the organic market. Add preservatives, and low nutrient topsoil and the plant loses even more nutritive value. Then we take this food and process it and it contains very little to sustain us. In fact, it creates a burden.

This would require a huge shift in some of our industries, but I really feel that these problems can be overcome with ingenuity coupled with a shift in consciousness. New opportunities will arise as the economy shifts, this change will not happen overnight; there will be time to adapt. The shift in consciousness can happen in an instant, but the logistics of this shift will occur over time. First we must yearn for the change, and I believe that some of us already do. We would feel it, if we were to just listen with our hearts. Anxiety, depression, addiction are all symptoms of the disruption of our path and the resistance to our expanding consciousness. Calm your mind and hold these ideas in your body. Notice how they make you feel, what are your reactions to the words I am writing? Now act on them. Please don't speak of sacrifice; we are currently sacrificing the youth of the future. We are sacrificing our current youth. We now have more people dying of being over nourished than undernourished, for the first time in the history of mankind.[7] If you want to talk about sacrifice, it has already begun. The sacrifice just hasn't been yours.

Water Supply

Water is the second converging emergency, and it could arguably be the most urgent. Right now we have two million people dying of waterborne illnesses every year, most of those deaths are children under 5.[8] All of our environmental issues are interrelated. Most of the issues with our water supply come from our devastating agricultural practices. Currently, there are several dead zones forming, the largest one in the Gulf of Mexico. As all of the agricultural waste products flow into the Mississippi, it creates an excess of phosphorous and nitrogen in the water. This run off eventually makes its way to the Gulf and causes large blooms of algae to form. This algae consumes the oxygen and leaves the water inhospitable to most other living creatures. The dead zone fluctuates in size depending on the levels of farming and the weather and it reached its highest point in 2011, spanning 9400 square miles.[9]

Without a more wide spread local movement that aims to support ourselves regionally, we cannot begin to deal with our water shortages and pollution. If you begin to buy locally, food operations will be much smaller and easier to maintain with little to no pesticides and herbicides. The use of smaller machinery will allow for less topsoil erosion, allowing for more of the nutrients to remain in the ground and less evaporation. Petroleum laden fertilizer use will be lessened, allowing for fewer toxins to go in the ground water. When only 2.5% of the world's water is fresh water, this is a good thing.[10] Many experts believe the wars of the future will not be over oil, but over water.

30% of our fresh water is ground water. Currently, about one quarter of the world's population is using groundwater in faster rates than it is being replenished, that is about 20% of the aquifers worldwide.[11] Some of the aquifers being exploited have been around for thousands of years. People are finding that their wells are drying up and it is forcing us to drill wells that go deeper and deeper into the ground. The water we do have available to us is becoming increasingly more toxic. Our bodies cannot live without water, it is the lifeblood of every living thing on our planet and it is something we take so for granted. We need to take a big step personally in our homes and globally, in terms of our agricultural practices. Using natural landscapes around our homes is something each of us can do to lessen the burden on our water supply. For example, the idea that we want green grass in a desert environment is the opposite of living in harmony with nature. I see a big trend towards this and that really gives me hope. A natural landscape can be beautifully done and requires very little water. Again, requiring no fertilizer to pollute the water system, no residue entering the house. We track in these chemicals on our shoes and carry them through the house, the fewer toxins that we bring into our environment the better. Also, if you can grow your own food, even a small garden goes a long way in boosting the food supply.

Energy

Many of the experts already believe that we have hit peak oil. This means that all of the cheap and easy to extract oil has been used and now oil becomes increasingly harder and more expensive to access. Now this idea of peak oil has been widely debated, but does it seem right that in a mere 200 years we may have used up half of the world's oil reserves that took millions of years to develop? Even if you can debate the numbers, does this seem ludicrous to you? Oil has led to the creation of our current society. Every aspect of society is deeply grounded in our use of cheap fossil fuels. We have seen the creation of suburbs that now requires us to drive a long distance to get to our place of employment. Now instead of walking, we drive everywhere. We use petroleum in many products from diapers, to plastic containers, to dish soap. We are over dependent on this energy source. So what happens if those experts are right and we are heading into a decline in oil?

We have already begun to see a shift in our energy extraction practices. The oil sands in northern Alberta and the use of hydraulic fracturing (fracking) are being increasingly depended on in the oil and gas industry. This is creating large-scale destruction to the landscape and they are devastating the environment. These practices also require huge amounts of water. It is estimated that a single fracking job uses anywhere from 1 to 5 million gallons of water.[12] To give you some perspective, the water used in the fracking sites in Colorado could provide water to upwards of 296 000 households for an entire year.[13] The oil sands are no better. They use twice the amount of water per year than the city of Calgary uses.[14] Calgary has a population of just over 1 million people.

To move forward, our focus will have to be one of conservation. Now under our current view of the world, conservation is synonymous with sacrifice. Once we release our attachments to material gain and move toward the riches of inner peace, conservation will be a choice without feeling like we are giving up something. According to the UN Global Compact, 20% of the world's population is using 80% of the world's resources. If you hold that in your heart space, how do you feel about knowing that you are in that 20%? Away from the fear, and the survival reflex, does it feel right once all of that is stripped away? In all truth it doesn't really matter whether you feel good or bad, the earth cannot sustain it much longer. Our population is too big, our earth's resources too finite or slow to renew and as more people thirst for our material consumerist based economy, the quicker the ecological decline will be.

No amount of alternative energy resources can maintain the status quo. One of the best ways to conserve energy is to live according to what your environment allows. If you can support a large population regionally, meaning you have the resources available to you, then build wisely, live conservational and communally. If you cannot support masses of people regionally, then we need to shift, make adjustments and expect less material goods. However, just by shopping more regionally, this will be reduced. There will be huge resistance to this by the multi nationals, but there again they have the ability and the means to adapt. Get your stores to provide services, but get them to seek out local dealers and products and operate from a smaller scale.

Maybe you are asking yourself how conservation helps your health and the impact is both direct and indirect. It is the indirect negatives that worry me. Human bodies are wired to react to immediate threats not seemingly longer-term emergencies. Unless we connect and move inward we can't appreciate the enormity of these issues. Without change, the depletion of food, energy and water will affect your health and definitely the health of your children. But it also has an impact in small ways in the here and now. What if you did more dishes by hand, instead of loading the dishwasher? What if you walked to the grocery store to pick up those few items instead of driving? What if you planted and tended to that vegetable garden instead of going to the grocery store? These are just a few of the examples, but all of them can promote health whether it is from an increase in your caloric expenditure, or contributing to community, or developing your sense of purpose. We need to start viewing our health in a much broader sense, when we are all connected – it all matters.

The Corporatocracy

The final component, which is a direct cause of many of pressing issues we face, is our trend towards a Corporatocracy rather than a democracy. This is a term defined by John Perkins in 2004, which describes a political and economic system driven by corporate interests.[15] When the policy makers are no longer beholden to the greatest good of the people, we see many laws that do not reflect sound public policy. Greed, complacency, and our short sightedness are what got us to this place today. The special interests and lobbies hold far too much power. Without reform to campaign contributions and the like, we will end up in a world where more and more policy is dictated by corporate and special interests. Corporations should not be seen as having some of the same rights as people under the 14th amendment of the Constitution.[16] This perhaps was one of our greatest errors. Now we have companies, in health care for example, that are beholden to the shareholders and not the people whose health they have in their hands. Their focus is on profits and not what is a good long-term decision for the people and the planet. The whole system is based on getting people to buy more, use more and sell more.

That is what people envy about the United States, it is not our wealth or power; it is the stuff or the ability to own stuff. This is the symbol deserving of envy. Currently, we are willing to peer with a blind eye for the illusion that the American Dream is attainable. The answer is not about more government or stricter regulations. Our government is increasingly corrupt, many politicians greedy and the system is flawed. In essence, we have created a monster that does not serve us. As individuals and as communities we need to consciously create something better. We can make a new agreement with ourselves and take the giant leap towards true freedom.

Right now there is a huge movement going on as I write this called, Occupy Wall Street. Many people have come to gather in cities around the word to express their frustration with the growing economic disparity. Many are crying out for Socialism, but those too, are chains. The shift has to occur within, we need to empathize with the plight of every human. To understand that your pain is my pain. Having government govern us in its current state will only lead us to Fascism. I don't think what people are looking for is to be controlled. They want freedom and that is why I think it has to start in each of our hearts and in each of our bodies. It is love that we want to spread - not rule. Do we want the government to choose for us? Is that the answer? We are stuck in the confines of our limited thinking. Get out of the box, and move towards a shift of which we have never seen before. We cannot use the same thinking that got us into this mess, to get us out of it.

If we are the only self-conscious beings on the planet, then it is meaningful that we are special. We used this advantage to create a vapid and shallow existence based on greed, status and stuff. We are consumers. Listen to the word consume. According to Webster's Dictionary, to consume is to do away with completely or to spend wastefully. In 2005, according to the World Bank, 20% of the world's wealthiest accounted for 76.6% of private consumption. The world's poorest 20% only accounting for 1.5%.[17] How one sided is that relationship, at what point do we give back or ideally refrain from taking in the first place? Take everything I purpose and hold it in your heart. Take the ideas and sit still with them. Move these ideas up and down your body with your breath and your attention. Does it feel right with your truest, most honest self? Does it feel right?

As we move into the next section of the book, I hope you will find hope in what I am writing. Each one of us needs to move inward. Ask yourself, do I have a purpose, do I live with joy and do I live with health? These are important questions and as you move through the next section, all of these self-care techniques will bring you closer to those answers. They build the awareness and the health needed to bring about a better world.

Part II
Moving From the Inside Out

Chapter 5

Stress, Perception and the Body

We will never find true health if we do not manage our stress. We need to create less stress, but there will always be things in our life that we need to manage. There are many definitions of stress, but the one that I connect with the most is stress occurs when perceived resources do not meet perceived demands. I like this definition because it recognizes that part of it, is how we perceive things. Our bodies will react whether or not there is an actual stressor if we think there is one. The second reason I like this definition is because it talks in terms of resources. See Chapter 3 Cultivating the Sustainable Self for more details on resource management. What do we have at our disposal? If time and our skills are seen as resources, how do we use resource management as a means to cope with stress?

One thing we do know is how our bodies respond to stress. This is a very tangible and physiological response. Hans Selye in his General Adaptation Syndrome says we go through three predictable phases when we encounter a stressor.[1] The first stage is the Alarm Phase, or what is commonly known as fight or flight. In this phase, the sympathetic nervous system kicks in and releases a myriad of hormones, primarily epinephrine & norepinephrine. This causes blood and oxygen to be shunted to the muscles causing them to become more tense and rigid as they prepare for an imminent danger. We also see an increase in metabolism, heart rate, breathing rate, and blood pressure. In this phase the digestive, reproductive and immune systems are suppressed to allow the body to deal with the immediate stressor. This is followed by the second stage, the Resistance Phase. Over a period of time the body will attempt to cope and bring the body back into balance and regain homeostasis. In this phase, the coping mechanisms are at full capacity and the fight or flight response becomes less effective. In the final stage, the Exhaustion Phase, the body's resources are now depleted. The immune system begins to break down and illness can now occur. In this phase the body may begin to have the same initial physiological response as occurred in the Alarm Phase, but now the situation becomes chronic and damage will result.

Think about how often stress is experienced as a gastrointestinal manifestation or how stress interferes with fertility? Do you often get sick during times of heavy stress? That is because, as mentioned earlier, all of those systems are suppressed during the stress response. The fight or flight response is very useful in the short term, but chronically the release of hormones, (especially cortisol and adrenalin) can depress immune function and cause damage to muscle tissue, impair cognitive and thyroid function, cause hyperglycemia and increase abdominal fat.[2] With such wide-ranging effects, stress needs to be addressed. In one study they looked at the effect of chronic stress on the immune system of caregivers for people with advanced Alzheimer's disease. In the study they gave the participants a small puncture wound on the arm. On average, the caregivers took nine days longer to heal than their matched control group who were not under the same amount of chronic stress.[3]

Stress Reduction & Elimination

Stress can be tackled it in a multitude of ways. We need to use techniques that relax the body. There are various methods of stress reduction and you have to find the right ones that fit you and your needs. Second, we need to find ways to avoid the stressor completely. This may require you to challenge the ways in which you have set up your life and daily routines. I cannot tell you how to change your day-to-day life, or how to create a more serene environment, but you will know what needs to be done once you create a calmer mind and body. The answers will be given to you if you seek them out. Finally, the way in which we appraise situations needs to be addressed. This again will only come with a certain level of self-awareness. How are your mind and emotions affecting the way you see a situation and yourself? Do you have faith in your abilities; do you have faith in God/Universe that there is divine timing? If you aren't aware of your triggers, and your associations that you make, it is hard to learn to reappraise a situation/person or emotion.

Complementary therapy often revolves around stress reduction. This is a key factor in healing and thus finding balance. Now understanding how stress can manifest itself physically, mentally, emotionally, it would make sense that a goal of complementary therapies would be stress reduction. Exercise, imagery, meditation, yoga, tai chi, and hydrotherapy are only a few of the many options out there to reduce stress. The key is finding which one works, what needs the outlet? Very often, we need multiple outlets to reduce and release pent up energy, emotion and stress. Finding the counter balance is often where people go off course. If you spend your day sitting then maybe a more vigorous exercise regime is what you need, complemented with a meditative practice. If you have a very physical job, then maybe you need not go to the gym and lift weights, but instead a quiet contemplative practice and a brisk walk. We want to strive for the Yin and the Yang, the male and female energies. The cycle from submission into domination and back again. It is only then that we create a space for awareness to be achieved - everything else is just autopilot.

It isn't just our bodies that need an outlet for stress. We have to give our minds an opportunity for creativity. Watching television is not an outlet for stress. It is just more input that has little value for our minds or bodies. Art, music and design are becoming less and less valued in society, but it is these things that raise our consciousness and bring us into balance. They are important for our development and as an outlet. Of course, if you are an artist then your outlets will be different. How do you make yourself whole, instead of a linear being?

How Do You Cope?

Another important consideration in stress reduction is our coping styles. There are three major ways in which we choose to engage in stressful situations. Do we choose to deal with our emotions, the problem directly or do we choose to appraise the situation always from the same perspective?[4] Some of us will choose to manage our emotions versus manage the situation. Emotion focused copers look at how the situation affects their emotions. These individuals would seek out ways to manage their emotions and perhaps take a more inward approach through meditation or guided visualization. Or maybe they get overly focused on their feelings and become a drama queen. They may also be the type of person who looks for and engages in support groups for the issues they are confronting. Take cancer for example, someone may look at dealing with the anxiety and fear that arises and will concentrate their efforts on dealing with those emotions versus the cancer directly. Remember in a system where all things are connected; improving one aspect bolsters the entire system.

On the other end of the spectrum, there are problem-focused copers. They would try to find ways to directly deal with the problem though elimination or by altering the issue. For these individuals they do research on the issue, develop action plans, or take steps to confront the issue head on. They are less concerned with the emotional impact of the problem and more concerned with elimination. Some may find comfort in the perceived level of control over a tenuous issue. The third way to deal with a stressor is the appraisal of the stressor. We all know people who have denial as a major force in their life. They may try to dismiss or deny the existence of an issue. Conversely, we all know people who look on the bright side of life, moving through things with a positive attitude; no problem is too large for them because they have the faith and security in their ability to handle challenges that may arise.

I had a woman in one of my classes on cancer survivorship who said, "God will never give me more than I can handle". A very common saying, but also a great adaptive strategy. Any issue she was presented with, even if she didn't know what she was going to do initially, she knew it was just a matter of time until the proper course of action would come to her. She truly knew that she was never given more than she could handle. Now that is a great appraisal coping strategy. It never ceases to amaze me how valuable a resource God is. She had faith in divine timing. There is so much never ending strength to draw upon and boundless wisdom if we just engage and be open to the possibility that we are divinely guided.

Another man in one of my classes was a classic engineer. Every problem he was presented with, he would list the strengths and weaknesses of the certain course of action. Whichever one seemed most logical in the end would be the course to take. I asked him next time he does this to become aware of his emotions while compiling the list. The next week he shared his experience and realized that he had a considerable amount of anxiety while putting the list together. This was a feeling that he had in the past ignored or had no awareness of. After being in my class and learning about stress reduction techniques, he began using them before and after the process. He said not only was he able to focus much better, but the answers as to the right course of action seemed much clearer to him. This is what happens when we approach life with a calm mind and open heart.

Awareness is again important when looking at coping

styles and dealing with stress. Generally, people prefer one coping style to another, but it is important to be aware of which one you use. The reason being, if a person relies too much on the problem, they may ignore the important emotional impact it is having on the body. If the anxiety, for instance, is ignored it can have real deleterious effects on the body. If a person only deals in emotional language, then they may miss some of the steps they could have taken to mitigate the issue. The person might just accept the situation as is, when there could be actions taken to avoid or eliminate the stressor. Awareness of where you fall on the spectrum will allow you to supplement your coping style, in other words, bring balance in another way. Since stress has a perceived component, the situation appraisal can be key in lowering the initial stress response.

Lifestyle and Stress

Even looking past coping styles, there are lifestyle factors that allow us to handle stress easier. I know from experience, that if I am not sleeping well, the world is much more difficult to deal with. I cry more readily and I lash out more often. Regular and adequate amounts of sleep are not only important for proper physiologic functioning, healing and repair, but also allow us to deal better emotionally and mentally. If we are talking in terms of creating the optimal healing environment, sleep is one of the most important things we can do for our bodies,[5] but we seem to be getting less and less of it. In my class that I teach on mind/body weight loss, we spend some time talking about sleep because certain hormones are released and regulated during our sleep. It appears that eight hours a night seems to be the magic number, any less and the optimal healing environment will not be achieved. The effect of hormones in weight loss is a complex matter and research is always coming out about what happens when there is a deficiency or when one shows up in excess, however we should be taking that research a step further. Why is our body not doing what it is supposed to do? Instead of getting caught up in the complicated details and interactions of the hormones. We should focus on promoting the optimal healing environment in the body. Giving the body the opportunity to heal itself. Please don't mistake me, there are certain circumstances where things are outside of our control, but if we work at bringing the body back into balance, it is wise and it knows what to do.

Being prepared for situations, doing research, allowing for enough time to get things done are also real life things that can make a big difference. I have met so many people in my life who constantly underestimate the amount of time needed to get things done. Consequently, this causes stress in my life and in theirs. Again if stress management is a balance between resources and demands, we need to be realistic about how much time (resource) it takes to complete a task (demand). I think we do this because we want to appease other people, but in the end it wreaks havoc in the minds and bodies of everyone involved. There is a great saying, "Lack of planning on your part, does not constitute an emergency on my part."

It is also important to have a strong social network of people that you can love and laugh with on a regular basis. As mentioned, social connection is very important in the appraisal of the situation. There seems to be a protective mechanism in having social support in regards to stress.[6]

Stress and the Mind

There has been a lot of research lately in a type of

psychotherapy called Cognitive Behavioral Therapy. This looks at how our negative thought patterns can be changed to approach a situation differently. It is commonly used to treat phobias for that reason. This type of cognitive restructuring is important for any change. Anybody who has worked with people trying to get them to make changes in diet and exercise, for example, knows that it is an uphill battle. This is because we rarely focus on changing those deeply engrained ideas, thoughts, beliefs and associations that we have about ourselves and our relationships to food and physical activity. For change to occur in the body, change also needs to happen in the mind. This requires a shift in the way a person perceives those changes, or they will always fall back to their old habits. One should never underestimate the power of those beliefs, conscious or unconscious.

Psychologist Albert Ellis and Psychiatrist Aaron Beck developed Cognitive Therapy to focus on the self deprecating, negative self-talk that we use on ourselves. As the field advanced, they began to include relaxation techniques such as biofeedback, thus creating the field of Cognitive Behavioral Therapy. In order to create change you must first be aware of the negative messages that we send ourselves. Then replace those messages with healthier attitudes and actions. The idea of affirmations used to be seen as the habit of New Age psychologists, but it creates some very real physiological correlates within the body. After all, if we know negative thoughts can change the physiology of the body, then wouldn't it follow that positive ones do as well? That is why right thinking is a component of the optimal healing environment.

Self-efficacy, or having faith in one's ability to complete a task is important in dealing with stressors regardless of the coping style. From a hypnosis perspective, all unknowns are seen by the mind as a negative.[7] Even if the issue or event is regarded as a negative, if the mind considers it a known negative then there is a decrease in stress. If there are unknowns, anxiety and stress levels rise in the body. When doing imagery for individuals prior to surgery, part of the process is taking them through the whole procedure, as well as doing stress reduction visualization. The reason for this is so the mind knows what to expect and knows what's coming. It is much easier to have faith in your ability to deal with a situation if you know what to expect. I host an online radio program and before my very first show I was extremely nervous. So nervous, in fact, that I broke out with three cold sores on my face. Cold sores for me are a classic sign of stress. My biggest fear was that I did not know what to expect. I did my due diligence in preparing for my show, but because I had never done it before I couldn't even anticipate what troubles I could encounter. So in this instance the best thing I could do was try to stay present and manage the stress.

Finally moving within and identifying fears, is a key component of stress and the mind. This is a hard one for us to do. We are so uncomfortable with being uncomfortable in our society. Again, it is an interesting dichotomy that on one hand we praise the incessant need to be busy which causes us misery and suffering and on the other hand we shy away from looking at the real fears of our inner most being. This is the resistance I was speaking of, and we are shying away from our heart's longings. When we don't look at our fears, anxiety begins to build just below the surface and ultimately, it creates an imbalance. Ask yourself, what are you really afraid of?

Every stress we feel, I contend that we look at head on. In fact, even write it down in a journal, put it on paper. Identify your fear and then physically remove your thought out of your body. In Christina Baldwin's book *Life's Companion: Journal Writing as a Spiritual Quest*, she calls this exercise "touching dragons".[8] Look at your fears head on, and most importantly follow them all the way through to the end of the thought. Then decide if the fear is mind made, and can be released. Or, is it an actual fear, based in reality and if so, how do you mange the emotions it creates? Is there an action you can take to mitigate the impact or can it been seen in a different light? Maybe as a challenge or as an opportunity for growth, rather than as a negative? Does the fear serve a purpose and is that purpose a healthy one?

For example, say a breast cancer patient is afraid of losing her hair during chemo. This is a very likely fear, not a mind made one. But what is she really afraid of? Is the root of the fear really death or fear of feeling less attractive? Only she can answer that. To manage her emotions she needs to do something to release stress. Maybe this is meditation, maybe it is massage, and maybe it is energy work. And now she needs to come up with an action plan as to what she is going to do when her hair is gone. Now this is a very personal choice. Perhaps, she would feel better getting a wig, or a scarf or maybe she can do what may other women have done and just be bald. The point of the exercise is to follow the fear all the way through and figure out how to deal with it. The mind is scared of the unknown and sometimes not addressing the fear all the way to the end causes greater stress than if we look at it head on.

How does being mindful help with this process? Since

the mind is such a major component of stress i.e. how we perceive things, then being in the moment is important. How often do we obsess about things that may or may not happen? Every time we do that our bodies react negatively and we begin the whole cycle over again. Our minds do not know the difference between a memory and an actual event. If our minds are in a chronic state of stress then our bodies will follow suit. A decision needs to be made about what things we can change, what things we can release and what things are out of our control. This can only be done once we have the awareness of what we are facing. This is where faith in ourselves and faith in others, perhaps even in God comes in. But if we can't connect with the moment and where our bodies are in time and space then we conjure up things from the past, or we worry about things that may or may not happen in the future. The past is already part of the present, so there is no need to lament or conjure up old memories over and over again. If we are in need of that information for a future decision, then the past will be there. There is no reason or requirement for us to bring it consciously with us for our memories are stored in every aspect of our beings from the cell to the biofield.

Stress and Emotions

In Buddhism, they believe that emotions are not to be controlled, but allowed and released. This process of surrender and release is healthy for our bodies and our state of mind. This does not mean that we ignore or stuff our emotions, rather the exact opposite. We face our emotions head on, sit with them and then when they no longer serve us, we allow them to float away. It is these attachments to the emotions that cause suffering and can even increase sensations of pain. Capturing emotions are like trying to capture a cloud, it is impossible. However we like to take the emotions and integrate them into our identity. Joseph Goldstein said in Insight Meditation: the Practice of Freedom:

"From a meditative perspective, various mind states, including emotions, arise and pass away empty of any substantial nature. They come into being when certain conditions come together and disappear when the conditions change. None of them belong to anyone; they are not happening to anyone.

In a very real sense each mind state or emotion is expressing itself; it is desire that desires, fear that fears, love that loves. Can you feel the difference between the experience of "I am angry" and "This is anger"? Through that little distinction flows a whole world of freedom."[9]

Emotions are not part of us. They are impulses of energy and their interpretation, identification and integration is our choice and a product of the ego. They allow for an experience and bring to light a circumstance, but they are not of us. Think of emotions as signals to your body. Become aware of why you feel the way you do. A strong emotional state is a message to the mind and body that there is an opportunity for growth and self-discovery. As with all things in life, emotions are impermanent and the more tightly we try to hold on to them, the larger our suffering. So the good, the bad and even the ugly emotions should be allowed to run their course. In terms of stress, it is the suppression and repression of emotion that has a negative impact on our physiology. A positive mental outlook allows for the free expression of all emotion, not just the positive ones.

Allow emotions to pass through you, surrender to them and then release them. So, when we are mindful or in the present it really allows us to let go of those anxieties that are mind made, they are ones that exist in either the past or the future. There is less long-term suffering, and therefore less stress response by the body because we are not attached to the emotions. That doesn't mean that those emotions won't be hard to deal with or lessened when you deal with them. In fact, the more aware you are of them the more intense they might be, but they won't continue to plague you in the future. Emotions allow us to experience the depth of a circumstance. They are part of the experience, but they are not part of us. We are not anger, or fear, or even happy. We are a person who feels happy and maybe the next day sad. Allow those emotions to be and then let them go. We are not giving in or giving up, we are letting in and then letting go. Again, there will be no release without surrender.

Dealing with our stress in an appropriate way is a key component of the optimal healing environment. We cannot be in a place of wholeness while at the same time under chronic stress. It creates an inflammatory response physically, creates unstable moods emotionally and decreases our ability toward creativity. In order to create true health and wellness, stress must be addressed.

Chapter 6

Holistic Fitness:

Being Mindful Through Movement

The physical body is more than the genetic outplay of physiological processes. It is the vessel from which this human experience…experiment gives life. No wonder we have gone so far away from health and healing and the knowledge of our own healing abilities. We see the gym as our means of physical expression, a scheduled chore that neither brings us true joy nor true health. One cannot exist without the other. Creative movement is integral in the healing of the physical body and creating the optimal healing environment. Creative movement is not just dance, it includes all movement, even those as simple as the fundamentals of existence i.e. washing the clothes, cleaning the house, growing our food and cooking our meals. We need to make our movement mindful, meaningful and purposeful for health to occur. For some reason we created spaces so artificial in nature and scope to move our bodies that we have missed the mark entirely.

Gyms to me, represent a symptom of our imbalance. We

created them to further deny our basic human needs and desires - just another way to create separateness from Spirit and each other. Our lives became so busy that we needed a place we could go three times a week to move our bodies in a purely unnatural fashion. It too is a symptom of resistance. We have a tendency when things are out of balance to take a Band-Aid approach instead of questioning the causes and the systems themselves. As our weight began to get out of control, we saw an increase in the promotion of gym type settings. Never asking ourselves, why are we getting fat? What have we omitted from our lifestyles and what have we added in, that has created this epidemic? Important questions that have far reaching answers.

Our bodies were made to move, to laugh, to love, to feel, express and explore. Running on a treadmill while watching TV removes us from this and disallows true human experience. There are of course times, like during rehab, and in time of limited functional capacity that gyms and therapy have a very real and valid place. Some people really like going to the gym and it works for them, but don't let it become your only outlet for your body. You are rarely ever being mindful when working out in the gym. As I mentioned, most of the time you are trying hard to take your mind off of the task at hand. That is why almost every cardio machine has its own personal television and a place for your magazine. We go to the gym, get the chore of moving the body over with and then go about the day in the same non-life giving ways that prevents healing. We need awareness and connection in order to be whole.

That being said, I think that there are some gym type settings that do things right. I belong to the YMCA[1] and I

Calories In vs. Calories Out:

An Incomplete Equation

Two-thirds of our population is overweight or obese. Even though weight loss is a billion dollar industry, we are fatter than ever. Weight loss is a complex issue and not fully addressed by calories in vs. calories out. How we view ourselves, our level of happiness in life and our self-awareness all plays a part. This is the essence of Holistic Fitness. When looking at weight loss, a person needs to look at the weight as a symptom of imbalance rather than the end game. The weight will always come back, if the underlying issue is not addressed. These issues will vary from person to person, but it is important to be consciously aware of where you are out of balance. Is it not dealing with stress, or maybe it is not getting adequate rest? Are your food habits way out of whack? Once you know those answers you need to ask yourself why? And what can you do to change them? Sometimes simply knowing or becoming aware of these conditioned patterns and programs that we run on is enough to make some big changes.

How do we accept ourselves when we are not perfect? We all experience things about ourselves that we would like to change, but we need to strive to find joy, even when we haven't met those expectations. How many times have you said to yourself, when I am thin I will be happy? When my life calms down, I can take some time out for myself or when I make more money I will have what I need to be joyful and healthy? We need to flip those declarations around to really create meaningful change in our lives. When you are happy first, then all other thing will fall into place. When looking at weight loss, positive choices will be easier to make once you find your happiness. You will shed old habits like a snake sheds its skin. Being happy, like all things in life, may be an impermanent state, but it is a goal worthy of your continued attention. If you do not make it a top priority in this moment, you will not make the adjustments necessary for enduring lifestyle change.

There are various ways to create happiness in your life; here are only a few. The first and most important is to live a purposeful life. Ask yourself, does my life have meaning? Do you move through life with goal directed behavior? Secondly, we need to be more aware of the negative and incessant self-talk that we say to ourselves every day. Cognitive Behavioral Therapists believe that negative thinking is not only related to depression, but can be the cause of it. What messages are you sending to yourself on a daily basis? The messages all have an emotional component, as well as a chemical communicator that has an effect on the body's physiology. Thirdly, we need to have a social support network. People who feel isolated have more feelings of depression and have less resilience to stress.

As with everything, we need to look at our weight holistically. It is not just about moving more and eating less. If this were the case, we would all be thin and happy, right?

see on a regular basis that they are consistently improving the services that they offer to their members. They are not about selling personal training sessions; they are really about providing for the needs of their community through accessible, inclusive programs aimed at the mind and body. They understand that there is heath and healing in group connection that is based on respect and kindness. The rise in popularity of the non-community based gym setting overall is more where I am directing this commentary.

I want to know what happened to nature? Where did we lose desire to be a part of it, to meld with it, to breathe it in? Again, we are moving further and further away from our true selves. Someone once said to me that we have all lost sight of what it means to have inner peace. He was right in so many ways. Some of us don't even realize that that is what we are longing for. So we fill this void of unawareness with food, drugs, etc. to close the gap. I have done it myself for many years. Avoiding my true self with drugs, alcohol and smoking. Always knowing that it felt incongruent and inconsistent with whom I truly wanted to be. But I wasn't ready to accept it and embrace it. I was in resistance.

The Five Principals of Holistic Fitness

How do we bring the mind and the spirit back into our physical activity? Exercise is an important component of the optimal healing environment. It should be a meaningful, mindful engagement of the body. There are five basic principles that I use to make physical activity more purposeful: breath, balance, nourishment, awareness and gratitude. Each one of these has a basis in physiology, but I feel each one has spiritual significance as well.

Breath

Ahh, the breath. It is one of the physiological processes in the body that can be completely automated, but also has a profound healing effect on the body if we change it from an unconscious process to a mindful one. Attention to breath should be just that, attention, not control or regulation. But by bringing awareness to it, we become mindful.

In Taoism, there is a flow to all things. This intelligence or flow of information moves through us. Again, it is the resistance to the Tao or flow that causes ill being and illness. In Exercise Physiology, we have something called Steady State, and that is when oxygen supply meets oxygen demands. I am sure that all of you have some idea as to how this feels. I attain this often when jogging. I reach a phase where I feel like I can go on forever. I have a perfect match between my demands and my resources, but I think that something much deeper is being achieved; I am finding my own rhythm, the Tao. A perfect harmonious balance between our breath and our bodies. This is a true expression of being present and allowing the free flow of spirit.

On a very pragmatic level, the breath has a nourishing effect on the body. Stress reduction and pain management are two of the biggest benefits of the breath, particularly diaphragmatic breathing. See the exercise on Belly Breathing on the Beach in the Appendix for instruction on this technique. This style of breathing has been shown to better oxygenate internal organs, increase energy levels and metabolic rate and revitalize stagnant areas of the body. The brain stem is the breath control area of the brain; it also serves to regulate other autonomic processes such as heart rate, breathing rate, blood pressure and skin temperature.[2] If we can learn how to self regulate some of these processes through awareness and practice, we receive a degree of autonomy over the healing actions of the body.

Deepak Chopra called this *conscious living*, the understanding that we can create change simply by bringing in awareness and shifting perceptions.[3]

It is so important to breathe during a workout. From a strength-training point of view, it is very important to exhale on the exertion point. This helps to decrease pressure in the thoracic cavity while doing the exercise. If you find this too hard to achieve, then maybe your weight is too much for you to handle. Again you can find your own flow during strength training. Find your breath, use your awareness and focus on the muscle or muscles that are being worked on. I always urge people to view strength training outside of the box as well; encouraging people to find their own rhythm and in doing so, making all movements have meaning and purpose. That is why yoga instructors focus so much on the movement of breath. Breath is believed in yoga to be the bridge between body and consciousness. If that is true, and I do think that it is, that is the bridge also to our understanding of our connectedness…..to Spirit. In yoga this is called Pranayama, Prana meaning life force and Yama meaning breath. A deep breath can oxygenate the body on a physiological level, but it also moves life force through our bodies and helps to connect us to each other. Once this awareness is achieved even on the most basic level, it is a profound healing and life giving tool that each of us has in every moment.

In all of life there are layers of awareness. We can look at things from the macrocosmic to the microcosmic and at times they seem to contradict, but I believe we just don't understand the science of consciousness enough to fully appreciate how they are connected. So to look at something like exercise and think it exists outside of Spirit would be foolish. In time, we will see that incongruence is not part of the true natural order of things and that polarity is no longer our natural state, it is time for us to move on.

Balance

Balance is a simple, basic concept, but perhaps it is the most difficult and the most detrimental to the healthy existence of the planet and the individual when it is not achieved. On every level the universe strives for balance. On a cellular level, cells move things in and out of the cell trying to bring balance of intercellular fluids and nutrients. Everything is moving cyclically and our cells are being created and dying off in perfect balance until the system gets overwhelmed and the balance is interrupted.

How do we find this balance within our physical bodies? The answer is simple.........nature, creative movement and self-awareness. Very often people who are Type A personalities lean toward competitive sport and recreation. Though they need an outlet for this Yang leaning, they also, and perhaps more importantly need to seek out Yin activities. A busy business woman with a strong drive may love to do yoga, but will do a style of power yoga because it is more of a work out. What she really needs is a calming restorative yoga to get the balance she desperately needs. 'Like attracting like' it becomes a positive reinforcement loop, meaning that it amplifies the response rather than returning it to the set point.[4] In the body there are a few examples of a positive reinforcement loop, such as vomiting, but largely the body maintains homeostasis through negative reinforcement and stabilization.

Again, we use yoga for a great example; your body weight can be the best weight you can use. Not only does it allow for the integration of breath, but also a person gets into touch with their body by moving it in and out of different positions. This helps to keep the muscles of the body balanced in their appropriate ratios. Muscular imbalances put the body at risk for injury. You have all seen those body builders who spend way too much time developing their chest muscles and little time on their backs. Their shoulders are rolled right over in a permanent hunch. Yoga on the other hand, lengthens and strengthens the body naturally. Now, are you going to be able to bench 200lbs just training with your body weight? Not likely, but why do we need to train ourselves for an artificial movement that never occurs in nature?

In my own life, my use of drugs, alcohol and smoking arose more out of denial of my true self. Like the universe saying to me over and over, do you accept your path? I could always feel this strong flow of energy trying to move through me and the only way I could cope with it was destructively. I had creativity trying so hard to flow through me and all I wanted to do was temper the flow. Exercise plays a big role in my ability to deal with the creative flow of life. We all need outlets and finding the right one takes self-awareness. It has only been recently that I have fully embraced my true path in life. Until now I have been living in resistance to my pure being. We are designed to flourish and thrive and finding balance for our physical bodies is so important in accomplishing that. Somewhere beyond all the commercials and lobbying for our attention, we know this. All it takes is for us to become conscious of it, become aware.

Awareness

Awareness is necessary for change, acceptance and surrender. These are all valuable traits when it comes to the health of our bodies and is absolutely necessary for changing a behavior. Most people are not getting enough physical activity in their day and they know it. Our bodies give us all the information we need, if we use our inner awareness. Too much stimulation and not enough solitude create a hectic environment within our bodies. It is hard to be self-aware with so much going on that captivates our attention. There can be no awareness without acknowledgement and attention.

How do we gain this awareness? Solitude and education. One is a very different process from the other; one requires a still state of allowing, while the other requires action and motivation. Imagine everyday you wake up and your mind is like a blank chalkboard. The moment you open your eyes you begin to fill this chalkboard with information, some useful, but most of it unnecessary thoughts, memories, regrets and anxieties of the future. Somewhere on that board are the words of your inner being or essence. Letting you know the status of your body, your health and wellbeing and your innermost desires. However, you can't hear those words or feelings because the board is so overcrowded with useless thoughts and unnecessary worries. In solitude, like during meditation, we clear the board except for those thoughts of your innermost being. In many cases there are no thoughts at all, only being. That's where healing lies….biologically, spiritually, mentally and emotionally. All the answers are there. In communion with God, all things are possible, all things are knowable.

Education is another good route to awareness. Once you understand something through learning, you then have the opportunity for contemplation. An action then reflection. Once you understand something it is hard to go back to ignorance. If you research the needs of your body and if you can educate yourself on the benefits of what you are doing, then hold that information in your heart center, you can change your habits. I really feel that if we can create awareness and make things tangible and meaningful when it comes to our health then we would choose differently. If we opened up our heart space and quieted our minds, we would see our health and our healing with such awareness that our choices would change in an instant. Our choices towards being active and eating better wouldn't be seen as a sacrifice, rather as a preference.

So once we have spent time in solitude and have educated ourselves on the health benefits of exercise and eating right, we have the awareness necessary to make the changes. It is unfortunate that some fitness professionals want to make physical activity elaborate and difficult. In truth, we just need to use our bodies more with purpose and joy. Most of all we need to walk. You will never train for a marathon or be a professional athlete by doing a walking program. This is the truth. But this book is about health and healing and the best thing we can do for our bodies is walk and participate more in the essentials of daily living. For persons with chronic illness, the ability to complete the tasks of daily living is what they strive for. You need to be physically active to get there. Even if that means you start by walking to the end of the block and back. Do small intervals and work up every day. Reward yourself in positive ways for your small achievements. In fact, to decrease your risk of most chronic illnesses all you need to do is get 150 minutes of accumulated moderate physical activity throughout the week. As well as include strength and flexibility training twice a week.[5] If you are a slow walker then accumulate one hour of walking over the course of the day. Walking is one of the best things you can do for your health and has the added neurological benefit of cross-patterned movement that initiates visual, tactile and proprioceptive stimulation.[6]

All physical activities can be mindful. Anytime you are paying attention to what you are doing, you are practicing mindfulness. When doing strength-training exercises, and you put your attention on the muscle that you are trying to activate, you get better motor unit recruitment. You've all had that experience when you learn a new exercise and your muscles shake. Then a week and a half later you can perform the movement smoothly. Now you might want to attribute that to increased muscle mass, but actually the muscle is just better at motor unit recruitment. Your body and your mind are getting better at communicating in regard to that specific movement and it also may be that your muscle memory is kicking in. As mentioned, your body, mind and energy field all store memories. A person who has never worked out will take longer to see results than someone who has previously been in shape. This is because your neuromuscular system remembers their interaction with each other. Focusing on the muscle you are working on allows for this, but it also can decrease your risk of injury. When your mind is in the moment, you can become aware of your form and proper form is crucial to making a good contraction of the muscle and lowering the risk of injury. See how something so grounded in mechanics can have spiritual significance?

Awareness is a fascinating and tricky thing. It comes in layers, like an artichoke; you peel away each leaf, moving closer and closer to the center. You may have had that experience where you have encountered something over and over and then one day it is presented to you in a slightly different way, which then opens up a new understanding. It resonates with your true being, the heart center. We need to become aware as to what is at the base of our suffering. There is a root cause of our poor health and to the impending environmental disasters…we have yet to wake up.

Nourishment

Nourishment is our next principal in Holistic Fitness. Is what you are doing now nourishing your body? Nourishment are substances necessary for growth, health, and good condition. I would argue that there can be activities as well as substances that provide nourishment - as nourishment of the mind and spirit is necessary for health as well. Nourishment is a key component in what I call diet awareness. This will be discussed in the next chapter.

Does running on the treadmill make you feel nourished? Maybe to some it does, or maybe we haven't thought about exercise in a different way than what society is presenting to us. And, maybe there is an issue with that in every aspect of our lives. We need to understand that socialization dictates our actions, but it is only a philosophy relative to the masses. We have so many options to choose from and we can choose differently. Everything we have created is part of our oneness; it exists as part of our collective consciousness and we all feel the "shoulds" that help to perpetuate the status quo. Carlos Castaneda wrote in his book Journey to Ixtlan, "We hardly ever realize that we can cut anything out of our lives, anytime, in the blink of an eye."[7] I believe this to be a truth. But, I don't think enough of us are awake or aware enough of this fact (yet) to make the change. Where one day we will move from a place of scarcity into abundance, to move from individualistic to communal, to really experience on a daily basis our oneness - to live the truth that we are spiritual beings.

Going back to nourishment and physical activity, we need to go back into nature away from these artificially created environments so we can experience and breathe in the natural world. This is what nourishes us, this is what saves us. Ask yourself, what will nourish me?

Gratitude

Finding gratitude amongst the strife has a positive impact. In the past twenty years or so, a new movement in Positive Psychology is starting to recognize how gratitude can shift our mental perceptions, how we appraise situations. The most important time we can use this tool is when things seem hopeless and helpless. Find something in those times to be grateful for, make yourself great! It is hard to lament and to wallow in the mist of appreciation. This doesn't mean to deny or suppress negative emotion, but allow that to move through you with the awareness and acknowledgement it deserves, however realize like any other mind state, that it too is impermanent. What strength can you draw upon, what part of your identity allows you to forge on with greatness? True strength comes from depth of character, find the aspect of yourself that best serves the situation and from that, find your gratitude.

Gratitude in physical activity can help you in several ways. First, by helping to rid yourself of old negative thought patterns when it comes to exercise. So many people have been programmed to think that physical activity has to be painful or exhausting to have an impact. Remember all we need is 150 minutes a week of accumulated physical activity to decrease your risk factors for almost every chronic illness. Even if in the beginning you are not enjoying the activity you are doing, you can be grateful for the impact that it has on the body. That requires an awareness of what it is accomplishing for you, but having that awareness also helps to make things more meaningful for you. The physical body is only one aspect of the equation, but is equally important to the others. Second, recognizing and being grateful about the ability of your body to move is transformational. We take for granted that our bodies allow the expression of our spirit. If you get out in nature the opportunities for appreciation are endless. Gratitude requires us to acknowledge that there is goodness around us; that has an impact in our own lives. This is another way to grasp our connectedness. We are whole, but we are also part of a much larger whole. Using gratitude can help us grasp our holographic nature. We are not part of nature, we are nature.

Physical Activity & the Healing Environment

Physical activity is important for so many reasons and critical to the healing environment. Next to diet and stress reduction, there is no other behavior that affects as many systems and dimensions of wellness. Mentally, emotionally, physically and spiritually; physical activity provides benefit. I know there have been times in my life, where I have been physically inactive for periods of time. I can remember looking at myself in the mirror and thinking, "I look fat, how could I let myself get here?" Then a few weeks later I started exercising again and I began to see myself in a different light. My body had not physically changed in those few short weeks, but several other things had. One, my locus of control shifted. I now felt as if I had control over my situation. Two, biochemically, exercise had a positive effect on my body and my mood. Third and possibly most important, I became aware of the shifts that occur when not being active. It changes me fundamentally.

Love on the Run

By now, you must know that I really try to encourage people to get all or at least part of their physical activity out in nature. I think that there are benefits beyond just the physical ones to being outside; however if you are going to exercise on a treadmill or stationary bike, there are ways to make that time more meaningful. Watching TV while exercising is not the way to go, so try doing one of these exercises instead:

1. Love on the Run: Next time you are running on a treadmill, turn the TV off and use this time to bring love and compassion to your fellow man. Visualize your heart center opening and sending love to every person in the room. Then expand your heart to reach everyone on the floor. Go room to room and visualize sending love to every person in the building. Then imagine holding the whole building in love. Then once you get good at that, send the love to your city, your state, the country and around the world. This not only helps you develop your

visualization skills, and your attention, but it will help create a better world.

2. Visualize your Success: Very often, I will use the time to visualize myself doing what I love and doing it well. For example, if I have a class to teach or a meeting coming up, I will visualize myself feeling confident and doing well. I will go through the whole event in my head, imagining myself with grace, ease and a sense of self-empowerment.

It is a really amazing feeling to do this; not only does your body feel stronger, but also it will help you to open up your mind and your heart. These are two quick examples on how to help create change in yourself and even the world. Doesn't that sound better than watching TV?

Your body also adapts to exercise in very positive ways. The heart is a muscle and the more the muscle is worked, the stronger and more efficient it becomes. This has an impact by lowering your resting heart rate and your blood pressure. It also helps the body become less insulin resistant, which is very important for people with Type 2 Diabetes. It has been shown to be as effective as medication in dealing with mild to moderate depression.[8] All systems seem to be regulated when the body gets a certain amount of physical activity. When the physiology of the body is optimal, we create a more stable environment from which positive behaviors flow.

It has been said by some that illness can be a gift. If that is true and so many of us are suffering, is it a gift to all of humanity? Our collective wake-up call that we can transcend all of this mess through the lessons we learned through dis-ease? I don't think that we need to suffer. We could have chosen differently, but we didn't and it is not too late to recover what we have lost. We have abilities beyond our current imaginations, but we are stuck by the perceived limitations and forgetting about the limitless potential of the mind and spirit. The more we take care of our bodies, the more we can understand this. Our bodies are our temples.

Holistic Fitness is about how we make our bodies fit inside and out. It is about moving beyond our limiting mindsets about what we think exercise should be. We do that by creating the awareness that it just isn't about our bodies. It is about giving the mind and the spirit an outlet, a way to affect change in the universe. Sets and reps have their place, but we really need to see beyond the box. Our bodies are the tangible form that allows our mind and spirit to manifest and express. This should not always be done in an artificial setting like the gym. We need more physical activity through creative movement, play, joy, expression and love. Our hearts will heal when we start nourishing them. Our mind will be quieted when we find balance and our spirits will be nourished with gratitude, giving us the individual awareness from which we can heal the planet.

The Importance of Play

As we age, we forget how much fun it can be to get down on the ground and explore the world from different levels. My son reminds me of this on a daily basis. I know that many of you do not have toddlers, so you may be out of the hide and seek phase, but even as your kids age you can still engage in unstructured, creative movement. When was the last time you moved just out of pleasure and pure joy? Whether it is throwing on some music and dancing around while singing into your broom or an impromptu game of Frisbee in the back yard, there are benefits to your health at any age.

As we get older, we tend to focus on structured, scheduled exercise, with movement so repetitious that we can do other things like watch TV or read a magazine while doing it. The joy of play comes from being in a flow consciousness. This requires us to be in the moment. When you watch children play, they are always completely absorbed in what they are doing. They never split their attention between lamenting over the past or creating anxieties about the future. And for that reason alone, it has incredible health benefits and promotes a joy-filled experience.

Creative, playful movement also affects our physiology and mental well-being. We live in a very structured, linear and logical world. Play gives our minds a creative outlet, and has been positively associated with happiness and learned optimism - both states, which lend themselves to better health outcomes.[9] Play centers are found in the most primitive areas of the brain, meaning that is has been a biological necessity since the very beginning of human development.[10] It also helps us cope with stress and we know that stress has vast physiological implications on all dimensions of our wellness. From a more pragmatic standpoint, it can add to your daily caloric expenditure and help you lose weight. Play is essential for the development of children, but it is also important for your development as an adult. Take time out of everyday to be silly and joyful, it is good for the body, mind and spirit.

Chapter 7

Food as Medicine, Whole Foods and the Holistic Perspective

The foods and methods of food production that are good for our bodies, are also good for our earth. Three holistic fitness principals lend themselves to the discussion about our food and diet: awareness, balance, and nourishment. I am not here to write a chapter on the ultimate diet; there are many other books out there on that. Besides, I think the ultimate diet is unique to each individual person. There are great guidelines, but no one way of eating fits all people. I am more concerned about diet awareness i.e. understanding how the food we eat affects the body, the animals and our planet.

Food Production: Another symptom of Imbalance

Too many people are out of touch when it comes to food production. The way our food is produced and then subsequently processed, is integral to our health. It is not surprising that Type 2 Diabetes is the number one fastest growing illness in the Western world. Documentaries such as Food Inc[1] and the Future of Food[2] are trying to get the word out there, but still we need even more awareness about our current methods of food production in order to see a change. We need to care more about where our food comes from. Our lives are tightly linked to the world around us, so much so that degradation to the earth and the animals is degradation to ourselves.

Okay, maybe I lied a little saying I didn't have an ultimate diet. I am a huge proponent of whole foods. A whole foods diet is not a fad; it used to be a way of life. Again, we can look at economics, globalization, politics, almost all systems out there - they are as interrelated to our food production, as our own unique human make-up. As soon as we started the mass production of food, we started to slowly kill ourselves and the planet. Many people would disagree with me and say I am being dramatic. I know that our current methods of agriculture allowed for a huge rise in human population, and many people subscribe to the thinking that bigger is always better. However, neither the current methods of food production or our rising population are sustainable. This is where people say, we started producing food cheaper, making it more accessible and easy to fit into our hectic lifestyles. Are you starting to see that it is all part of the problem? We made the food more convenient, less nutritious, more harmful to the earth and more conducive to living life out of balance. We are doing the same Band-Aid job with the food system that we are doing with our health. As another symptom of imbalance rears its ugly head, we find yet another way to Band-Aid the situation instead of challenging the systems we have put in place.

It is undeniably true, we did see a giant leap in food production with use of chemicals in our farming, (erroneously dubbed the Green Revolution), but at huge environmental and health costs. Today the yield response to the increase use of fertilizer has slowed and is beginning to show signs of leveling off.[3] We also began using less and less diversity in the types of crops we were planting, which allowed natural pests to flourish. So what was our solution? It wasn't to go back to the root of the problem, but instead we starting using harmful pesticides to kill the ever encroaching pests while genetically engineering the food to contain genes that will kill them. We also started seeing opportunistic weeds in the lack of eco diversity and poor soil conditions, so our solution again was larger inputs of herbicides and more genetic modifications. Though there is still debate on yields, these huge industrial farms are around 25% less energy efficient than organic farms, due to the fact that they rely heavily on large machinery, chemical fertilizers, pesticides and genetic engineering to reach their yields.[4] Organic farming methods are more resistant to drought, maintain healthy topsoil and use the natural biodiversity to solve many of their issues. People have been farming organically for thousands of years and have only just begun to introduce the use of pesticides since WWII.

Does this mean I am promoting vegetarianism? No. Again, there is no one diet that is right for all people. I was a vegetarian for a year, and I was incredibly out of balance. I know a lot about diet and proper nutrition for a plant based diet, but it was not right for my body. However, that doesn't mean we need to consume meat at every meal or even everyday for that matter. I do think for our earth's sake, there will come a time (and that time is basically upon us) when the mass production of animal products will become too resource heavy for us to bear, and not to mention environmentally hazardous, but I am not against eating small amounts of sustainably produced meat. There has been a large rise in animal consumption; in the 1960's the average person ate 17kg of meat per person per year. In 2005, the average consumption was 40kg/person, which is over 260 million tons of meat. Thirty-eight percent of the world's grain goes to produce animal feed, and that doesn't even speak to the heavy inputs of water or the fact that grazing leads to soil erosion.[5] Our methods of food production must change if we want to see a change in our health, and in case you haven't noticed our health is failing.

Chronic Illness: Putting the Pieces Together

Let's talk briefly about Type II Diabetes, as this illness is not only being diagnosed more and more in adults, but in children as well. It is an interesting illness; as experts estimate that it could be prevented in about 90% of all cases.[6] Our body's normal response after we eat a meal is to increase the amount of insulin production by the pancreas; this serves to decrease the level of blood glucose by getting the glucose to the cells for energy. In the case of Type II Diabetes, the body becomes increasingly resistant to insulin or does not produce enough insulin to adequately do the job, therefore the body's blood glucose levels remain high. Over time, excess glucose in the blood can cause damage to eyes, kidneys, nerves or heart. Processed foods create huge spikes in blood glucose levels and over time the body becomes insulin resistant and the body's ability to deal with those spikes decreases. Add to that the weight gain, hardening of the arteries, high blood pressure and you begin see the breakdown of many systems. We have termed this as Metabolic Syndrome, as many of these conditions feed into one another.[7]

Our foods are being manufactured and engineered rather than grown and cultivated. Our bodies were not designed to eat processed foods. In addition to the insulin resistance, it puts a heavy burden on our liver trying to break down all the pesticides, synthetic chemicals and food additives. The food dyes, preservatives, food enhancers, hormones, antibiotics and pesticides are wreaking havoc on the body's detoxification system which includes: the skin, lungs, GI tract, kidneys and liver. The liver, which carries the brunt of it, goes through two phases in the breakdown of toxins. The first phase breaks down the toxin through the use of enzymes. This process creates bi-products that need further detoxification. In phase II, the body tries to remove the bi-products through bile and urine.[8]

High fructose corn syrup is currently being studied as a major risk factor for Metabolic Syndrome. Researchers at Princeton found that when they gave rats high fructose corn syrup they were more obese, had higher levels of abdominal fat and more circulating triglycerides than rats given sucrose.[9] We are the fattest we have ever been as a nation and it is not only because of larger portions and more sedentary lifestyles, but also because we aren't eating real food - whole food. We are eating food from a box instead of straight from a field. If disease is resistance, then we can see no better example of resistance than with our processed food and it's effect on the body. Again, in terms of creating the optimal healing environment, we need to support the natural processes in the body. In fact, carrying excess weight leads to inflammation as well because the fat cells themselves are active participants in inflammation. We now have a test to measure the amount of inflammation in the body called the C-Reactive Protein Test.[10] I would urge you to have that test done if you are suffering from a chronic illness. Stress, toxicity and most importantly our diet, plays a huge part in creating chronic inflammation.

Can we go back and remember why food keeps us alive? The food which should be grown in a nutrient rich soil, infuses the plant with the nutrients, which we then eat and get the nutrients introduced into our own systems. Those nutrients, then in turn are used as the building blocks for all metabolic and enzymatic processes in our bodies. If our bodies do not receive the nutrients they need, then our body's systems begin to break down. In processed foods, many if not all the nutrients are leached out in the act of processing. To add insult to injury, we are not only missing out on the nutrients, but all sorts of dyes, pesticides, additives, hormones, antibiotics and chemicals are added to the food, which we then ingest into our bodies. Our bodies are not designed to deal with those artificial substances. Some of you will read this and say "duh", but so many people haven't thought of food this way. If that were the case, wouldn't have chronic illnesses running rampant in the Western world.

Fat, proteins, carbohydrates, minerals and vitamins are all broken down into the building blocks that are used for energy production and all the processes carried out by the body. What do all the other added ingredients on the back of the box do for us? Are they just benign ingredients or do they block nutrient absorption and add to the already toxic burden we carry? In fact, some of the things

> ### Is Fat an Organ?
>
> Many people think that fat is simply excess tissue that just accumulates from a poor diet and lack of exercise, but in truth it is much more than that. Fat is actually very active. It plays an important role in the healthy functioning of the body, from a woman's reproductive system, to metabolism and immune function. So if we think about fat in its true role, what does having large amounts of excess do for our body?
>
> Scientists are discovering more and more the complexity of adipose tissue. To give one example, fat cells produce a substance called Leptin. Leptin is a hormone involved in regulating hunger and satiety signals in the body. In a healthy state, Leptin is closely regulated, so as fat tissue begins to increase there is an increase in the release of Leptin, which then tells the body that it is satisfied. This signals the body that it is no longer hungry, thus bringing the body back into homeostasis. When a person becomes very overweight, they become resistant to the Leptin being produced by the body, so the signals of satiety are not being sent. Leptin, when unregulated, also seems to be a mediator of inflammation in the body. Obesity and inflammation are very closely linked.[11]
>
> Chronic inflammation is thought by some to be the underlying cause of all chronic illness including, arthritis, cancer, and heart disease. Inflammation is an important part of the healing response in the short term, but when it persists, it begins the breakdown of the body's systems.

that we add have no nutritive value and they are neurotoxic, meaning that they kill brain cells because of their excitotoxic effects. When you eat excitotoxins, like monosodium glutamate (MSG) and aspartame for example, it stimulates the brain to release glutamate in excessive amounts; this neurotransmitter lingers in the synaptic gap (the space between two nerve endings) and causes cell death and nerve damage.

Another result of eating a diet heavy in animal protein and processed food is that it creates a highly acidic environment in the body. The acid/alkaline balance is critical to maintain and the Standard American Diet (or SAD and it is very sad), is very acid producing. Have you ever wondered why as a nation we consume some of the highest amounts of calcium through our intake of dairy products, yet we still have very high incidence of osteoporosis? It is due to the high pH of the foods we consume. In order to maintain a sustainable pH in the body, it forces the body to leach valuable minerals such as potassium, iodine, magnesium, sodium and calcium to compensate. These minerals have very valuable functions in the body and should not be used to maintain a healthy pH level. When the body is forced to do this, the systems in the body that are regulated by those minerals no longer function optimally. For example, iodine is essential to the proper functioning of the thyroid gland. The thyroid gland is largely responsible for our metabolism. If the iodine is used to maintain the pH balance then the thyroid can become sluggish and lead to weight gain.

Food as Medicine

We need to view food as medicine and thus, it should be our first and foremost means of addressing illness. Again, if resistance creates disease, how are our bodies reacting to the food we are eating? Could it be, it is resisting? Our digestive system is very efficient if it is kept in balance and given things it can utilize. More over our bodies are incredibly capable of self-correction if it has all the proper building blocks. Changing your diet can be the most important thing you can do for your body.

Dr. Dean Ornish did a landmark study where he found that people were able to not only slow down the rate of their heart disease, but also reverse it by eating a plant-based diet.[12] Dr.Ornish's program for reversing heart disease includes a stress reduction component as well as physical activity. He is one of the most forward thinking doctors that we have today. The most interesting thing that he found was that the bigger the changes that were made, the larger the positive effect on health. So, for the people who only made slight changes, they only received slight benefits and for those that went big - they were handsomely rewarded for their efforts. This should give anyone who is reading this with a chronic illness hope; you can change your health. Even the term chronic illness, suggests a long-standing commitment to being sick. How many of you have been told, you are going to just have to live with it? I say, I don't believe that to be the case. Ultimately all healing is self-healing. The real question is, are you ready to make the big changes needed? Are you ready and willing to be healthy?

As of late, we have put too much emphasis on genetics. Once again taking away our personal responsibility and self-control, giving away our power to deterministic factors. There has been promising research in Epigenetics from Dr. Bruce Lipton who says that each of our cells has a receiver and we are receiving messages that come from outside of the cell.[13] This means that genes can be turned on and off by environmental stimuli, for example through thought, feelings and emotions. Gene expression can also be altered by diet; if we regard food as our medicine and eat accordingly, we can lessen the need for detoxification and put our energy into being creative, productive and healthy beings. On one hand, there is a perspective that everything is predetermined and on the other, that humans are a dynamic ever creating system. That is the interesting thing about life and existence; there are so many theories and perspectives, which one do you choose to subscribe to? Because make no mistake, you make a choice, even if it is an unconscious one.

Are You Being Nourished?

Everything has an essence, which is true for all living things including plants. That essence is passed on to us when we consume it - it is part of the energy that exists in all things. We will get more into energy in later chapters, but through food processing we lose that energy transfer as well as much of the nutrient transfer. This serves to widen the disconnect between all living things. It dampens our consciousness. Next time you eat fast food, I want to you ask yourself immediately after the meal, how do you feel? Even if the answer is, "completely satisfied", then what about the food makes you feel satisfied? Then check in with yourself 30 minutes, an hour later, and two hours later. Ask yourself, do you feel nourished? Take a moment and check in with yourself after every meal for a week; use some inner awareness and pay attention to how it made you feel. These are the connections we need to start making if we are going to create change.

I hear a lot from students and clients that say they don't like the taste of vegetables. But what if we shifted our perceptions of food? What if we used education, gratitude, research and most importantly self-awareness to re-frame our ideas of what is good? Our bodies are out of balance, moreover they are in resistance and we know what needs to be done, at least I think we are starting to. Now we just need to create the space in ourselves where we begin to long for it. Once you understand what it means to be nourished, it is hard to go back. Once we understand the devastation that the mass production of cheap, nutrient deficient food has on our earth, the choice, and therefore the switch to healthier, more sustainable food will be easier. The foods that we once hated will actually begin to taste better. All things will shift from our preferences to our perceptions and this will ultimately lead to new choices made without sacrifice.

Our power can even extend beyond our health and our bodies. Our purchasing power, or the way we spend our money, gives us a daily voice in how the economy and thusly, how the country is run. But this will require change and dare I say it, initially sacrifice, until our consciousness and spiritual awareness surpasses our lust for technology and the quick fix. The fast food companies of the world, the mega corporations that basically run the entirety of our economies, will resist this notion. But, we have purchasing power, ingenuity and a strong drive for self-preservation on our side. But if we don't get our connectedness to the environment, then the shift will be abrupt, hostile and devastating. It will occur as we begin to run out of food, fresh water and other resources. Very rarely do we make good decisions under high stress and poor conditions.

Chapter 8

Our Toxic Burden:

What Can We Control?

I always find it interesting how we have chastised smokers, casting them aside because of their harmful behaviors. This is an arbitrary assault. When I lived in Vancouver, BC I used to take public transportation daily. There were many instances where the smoker would be getting dirty looks or a fake cough from another bi-stander, all the while there were three diesel buses idling right beside them. There are so many toxins and it is not that I think second hand smoke is good for you, but again our attack is rather capricious.

In most conventional medical circles, they say it is completely unnecessary to detoxify the body because our bodies are efficient and designed to do this. Which was true in the past, but now we are not taking into consideration the degradation of the food supply, the increase of environmental toxicity and increased stress levels in day-to-day life. In the last 200 years and since the dawn of industrialization, new and ever changing toxic substances are bombarding our bodies. Have you thought recently about what you are putting on your body? From make-up, to shampoo, to lotions, and sunscreen, we are literally smearing harmful chemicals on our bodies that require filtration and detoxification. Now, consider all the chemicals you use to clean your environment; from hand sanitizers to anti bacterial soaps to harsh chemical cleaners for the tub, shower and mirrors. All of that can end up in our bodies and this is just the stuff we opt to use, not to mention the chemicals we ingest unknowingly in our food supply and breathe in from our environment.

Now the point of this chapter is not to get you feeling like your life is out of your control, but instead to make you realize how much is within you. You have many choices as to what you want to use in your home and on your own body. Actually, it is with personal care products that I would like to start this discussion. As with many things, the underlying cause of our behavior is a result of fear. We are allowing this lie of outer beauty and of aging, to convince us that we need more. That our true beauty isn't enough; that the simplest things require additions of large amounts of make-up, perfumes, lotions and dye jobs.

The Cost of Beauty

We are in love with an artificial idea of beauty, one that is truly only skin deep and externally available. If you had a deeper connection with your spirit, and understood that we are all radiant beings of light, the external façade would have much less meaning. All the Botox, silicone and collagen that we use might seem a little unnecessary. I like that line in Avatar[1], where they look at each other and say, "I can see you". Maybe we use all of the technologies to prevent people from really seeing us as we see ourselves. Maybe aging wouldn't have such an impact if we were less resistant to flow, if we weren't so toxic physically, mentally, emotionally and spiritually? Consider the idea that aging is more of a symptom than a disease. Maybe toxicity, over indulgence of nutrient deficient food and lack of physical activity are enough to spur on aging by turning on the genes that are responsible for the aging process. Either way, if the body is toxic and the flow of life force is stunted enough to disallow the expression of the mind and spirit, we are in trouble.

Experts estimate that the average person puts on approximately twelve personal care products a day. That could mean that we unknowingly smear up to 170 chemicals on our largest and most porous organ each and every day.[2] If you don't find this alarming, you should. Next time you are getting ready, I want you to flip the bottle over and look at the ingredients. How many ingredients on there can you pronounce? Do you know what they do? I was having a conversation awhile back with my cousin and at a time when I was just learning about this stuff. We were in her bathroom and looking at all the ingredients on the bottle. There was some form of paraben in almost all of the products we looked at. We thought at the time, well this must be something used for sheen or for moisturizing, but in reality, it is a preservative. Now the data on parabens in still inconclusive, but a study done in England found trace amounts of parabens in nineteen out of twenty breast tumors.[3] The thing about personal care products is that the ingredients used are not generally tested for safety. According to the FDA, cosmetic companies can use whatever ingredients they wish in their products.[4] The industry is self-regulated, and if something does happen to be studied, they never look at the cumulative effects or the compounding effects of multiple products. There just seems to be a complete lack of regulation and research.

So, I am not advocating that we don't wear any make-up, but again be mindful about what you are putting on your body. If you are suffering with a health issue, do not over look the topics in this chapter as an exacerbating or source cause of your issue. Find products that are less toxic and most importantly, relying less on beauty products to derive your worth. And remember, where you spend your money is where the market will go. American cosmetic companies have already reformulated many of their products for European markets because many of the ingredients they use in America are banned in the EU. So, if we suddenly are looking for less toxic products, they will become available. Where are you choosing to spend your money and on what products? You can choose what you want to put on your bodies and what chemicals you want to clean your house with. These choices not only have purchasing power, but will help clean up the planet. The earth and you body will thank-you for it.

Our Toxic Homes

Let's look now at the toxicity of the home. From black mold, to Volatile Organic Compounds (VOC's), to the air fresheners, soaps and cleaners, there are a lot of things to consider. The EPA says that the concentrations of VOC's can be ten times higher indoors than outdoors. VOC's include everything from the paints, cleaning supplies, pesticides, building materials, furniture, office equipment, to glues and permanent markers.[5] The list is lengthy and they have been proven to create health problems, especially in sensitive individuals. So scan your home, what can you do to cut back? One of the easiest things you can do is use natural cleaning products. Substitute your window cleaner for a mixture of vinegar and water. One of the most effective soap scum cleaners I have found is white vinegar and baking soda. Cheap, clean and non-toxic. When it goes down the drain, it is not polluting the river and most importantly I am not inhaling harsh fumes.

Throw out your air fresheners, your highly perfumed clothes detergent and your anti-bacterial soaps and anything that lists fragrance on the back of the bottle. The ingredients in fragrance do not have to be listed and they can be a toxic soup of synthetic chemicals. You don't need them; they aren't improving your day. They are harmful to your body, and to the earth. Recently, the ingredient triclosan, which is used in antibacterial soap, has been shown to be harmful to humans. It seems that the ingredient breaks down when exposed to chlorinated water and produces toxic chemicals including chloroform.[67] I am sure you are thinking, but people wouldn't be putting things into the products that have known harmful effects, right? Currently on the market, there are over 82 000 synthetic chemicals being used in our products, many of which have not undergone any form of safety testing.[8] The legislation called the Toxic Substances Control Act, which governs many of these chemicals, was created back in the 70's and has not been revised since its creation.[9] You need to be your own advocate, research and educate yourself on what all those ingredients do to you and your loved ones.

Back to the Food

What about our food? Depending on the amount of processed food you eat, whether or not you buy organic,

HEALING ENVIRONMENT

you might be ingesting hundreds of synthetic chemicals everyday. Pesticides, herbicides, insecticides, fungicides, preservatives, food colorings, and flavor enhancers are just a few. These things are not well researched and nobody has ever looked at the cumulative effects of these substances over time, or if all of them together create a unique response in the body. But, let's use our common sense for a moment. If these substances are not essential nutrients, not being used for any of the metabolic processes in the body, should we be ingesting them?

Heavy metal toxicity is another source of toxicity that needs to be considered. Metals such as lead, mercury, cadmium, chromium, nickel, tin or arsenic are some of the more common ones. There are many sources of heavy metals from our fillings, to fungicides and pesticides, to pollution in the air from mining and coal powered power plants, to the fish we eat. Many of these heavy metals in small amounts are important to the proper functioning of our systems, but in large amounts can cause serious health problems and disastrous environmental concerns. Heavy metals can interfere with the proper functioning of the nervous, digestive and respiratory systems.[10] There are treatments available to detoxify from heavy metal toxicity, one being Chelation Therapy. Chelating agents are introduced into the body either as an IV, cream or taken orally. The agents bind with the heavy metals and aid in the removal of the toxins from the body. Infrared saunas can also be used regularly to aid the body in expelling its toxic load.

The Bigger Picture

An interesting way of looking at things is there are

Non-Toxic Ways to Clean Your Home

Have you given thought to the products you use to clean your home? As mentioned, it is important to remember that we need to be cautious of the harsh chemicals we are using to get the job done. These chemicals cannot only be absorbed through the skin, but can also be inhaled causing damage to the lungs. Here are a few non-toxic ideas for cleaning your home:

All Purpose Cleaner

Add 2 cups white vinegar and 1/8 cup baking soda to an empty spray bottle.

Add 2 cups of water and 18 drops of tea tree 100 percent essential oil (or the same number of drops of lavender or lemon 100 percent essential oil). Both the vinegar and essential oils act as a disinfectant.

Window Cleaner

Mix equal parts water & white vinegar in a spray bottle.

Hint: fold a clean towel into fours. Spray the area and wipe with a dry side. This will prevent streaks.

Soap Scum Remover

Sprinkle baking soda over tub and tiles. Spray with mixture above. Use a soft brush and scrub bath while mixture is still foaming. For tougher jobs use full strength vinegar.

about 1.2 billion people in the world that are undernourished or impoverished. Conversely there are about 1.2 billion people in the world that are over nourished, meaning overweight and overindulgent.[11] The first group of people are still dying of diseases from widespread infection through the water and unclean living conditions. The second group, which a lot of North America and Europe fall into, are people who are not dying of poor conditions, but poor choices. These are not just choices of unhealthy food and lack of movement, but also all the stuff we created to make our society more civilized. This is where most of the chronic diseases fit in.

What drives us to such extremes? The disparity is growing larger on a planetary scale, but also within our own country. Why are we choosing what we are choosing? Why are we choosing to live our lives so out of balance? We have a drive towards eating, drinking and creating things in our lives that are incredibly unhealthy. We know in our minds that they are bad for us, but why do we choose them over and over again? I think it is not only because we are out of balance, but as humans we are barking up the wrong tree entirely. Our focus is on the external, material world. We know in our hearts that there is something wrong with that, though it hasn't risen to our level of conscious awareness. Our focus instead should be on minding our spiritual and internal selves. We should have a focus on God/Source/Spirit and a striving for inner peace. This is the tree we should be climbing. Somewhere in our psyche we know this and that is why it is so easy for us to focus on the external. We are trying to push away what we know is true. In the meantime, we are doing disastrous, unspeakable things to our planet and each other.

There is a saying that we are only as strong as the weakest amongst us. I would argue that the over nourished are equal to the under nourished on the criteria of weakness. Perhaps even more so because we are blinded by our sense of entitlement and greed, even if the greed is more unconscious than not. In fact, the more "civilized world" might even be more toxic with the advent of all the new chemicals and pollutants. In 2005, the Environmental Working Group, looked at the umbilical cords of 10 randomly selected newborns in the United States and found a total of 287 chemicals and an average of 200 chemicals per baby.[12] Many of these chemicals are known to be cancer causing, interfere with the nervous system and cause birth defects. These pollutants are killing us, regardless of which end of the spectrum you fall. According to the World Health Organization, it is estimated that 70 000 Americans and three million worldwide, die every year due to air pollutants[13], mainly as a bi-product of energy production. When is enough, enough?

It would be so convenient to shell off blame on big evil corporations or lack of government control, but it is you and me and every person on the planet who has to rise up and be accountable. We are all responsible. This is not about giving up hope or self-loathing. It is about the awareness that the power for change lies within. In our hearts, in our minds, in the spirits of the communities and the world. Our government is the product of our lack of interest and accountability in the process.

We have been buying into this lie that are homes, hands and bodies are not clean enough or beautiful enough. This 'throw away' civilization is convenient, but toxic to our bodies and our environment - we are enough. We are abundant beyond our wildest dreams. It is only when we are over-grounded in our material, physical reality, that we can justify the illusion of scarcity. It is not the make-up, the hair or the designer fashions that make us worthy. We are powerful, divine beings of light. Let's be conscious beings and use our power productively.

Part III
Calm Mind, Calm Body

Chapter 9

The Mind/Body Relationship

If you imagine your life was a movie, your mind would be the director. In a movie, the director helps to direct all of the actors and film crew and he tells them what to do. He holds the grand vision. And as with a movie, there is a script. What is the story that is being told? Is it the story of a hero overcoming all odds or the downtrodden victim who always seems down on his luck? Who are the supporting characters? We follow scripts all the time, but the important consideration is whether we direct and even rewrite the script or whether the script directs us? Are we conscious or unconscious? We are the creators of this moment. We can direct our bodies towards healing or we can steer them towards disease.

Our minds have the capacity to make us ill and also to help make us well. Now that we understand stress, we know that how we perceive things affects the physiology of the body and that this perception adds to the uniqueness of the human condition. For what one person perceives as an obstacle, the other person sees as a challenge. This distinction can create a different environment in the body. The mind/body relationship is a powerful driver of our health. It is important to note that while your mind is an important part of the equation, it is a tool and it should be utilized as such.

Mind/Body Medicine (MBM) is becoming an important part of Integrative Medicine. For a long time we dismissed the working of the mind and strictly focused on how to alleviate the physical symptoms; this was to our detriment. However, with the relatively new field of research called Psychoneuroimmunology, we are really beginning to understand the impact of the mind on the physical, emotional, mental and immune systems of the body.

The mind can be an elusive topic. We mainly think of the mind as being synonymous with the brain, but it really encompasses much more than that. It includes our beliefs, our thoughts, our imagination and our conscious and unconscious awareness. The interplay between our minds and our bodies is beautiful in its complexity. Not only can we change the body with our thoughts, but we can change our mind by the actions of our bodies. For example, exercise has the ability to grow neurons. This is called neurogenesis. Scientists have seen that exercise seems to increase the amount of newborn neurons and although the exact effect of this is unknown, they believe it plays a roll in memory and learning.[1] We used to think the brain and its interactions were not plastic, but now we know that that isn't the case. Neurons may not have the regenerative capabilities that some other cells have, but we can and do have the capabilities to create new neural pathways.

This elegant dance of the mind and body teaches us many things. First, that our thoughts do have power, and I would argue in later chapters, even energy. Second, the more we make our thoughts conscious, we can change the physiological reactions of the body. Third, when we make more thoughts conscious, we can learn to change our behaviors, as always, seeing that minute changes affect larger outcomes and vice versa.

What Do You Believe?

Part of the optimal healing environment requires us to use what I will refer to as right thinking. This doesn't mean positive thinking, though that is definitely part of it. It means that our thoughts, and more importantly our decision-making are conscious, contemplated, explored and altered, if necessary. Right thinking is key to maintaining our good health and to initiate and enhance our own healing abilities. If you also have the will and the imagination to see and engage in the interaction of the spirit, these abilities will one day become limitless. I have a grand vision for the human spirit, one that requires a complete ejection from the box that we hold ourselves in, but we need to overcome the mental constraints that we have created and opt for something greater. As Willis Harman said, "The only limits to the human mind are those we believe in".

That is the trick with the mind. Many spiritualists will say that we should disregard the workings of the mind as it tricks us, with our ego always at the forefront of every decision. I would, in part agree with this, but I think through awareness the egoic mind can be overcome. The mind can trick us, there is no doubt, but that does not negate the importance that it has on our health. This is why I always tell people to view all things with a calm mind and an open heart. When the mind is calm and the heart is open, we do not fall prey to the ego. Though the ego can be our greatest teacher, for healing purposes it is necessary to see beyond it.

Through research we have seen profound examples of just how powerful the mind is over the functioning of the body. In many of these instances, the mind is not in a calm state, but they serve as useful examples. It is important to grasp the sheer power of the mind. We have seen in studies done on people with multiple personality disorder how complex the mind is. Different physiological conditions can exist in the same person. For example, people have documented different resting heart rates in the same person depending on which personality was in control.[2] Resting heart rate is a pretty stable measurement and is usually only altered over time and with exercise training. We have seen Blue Cross in California give guided imagery CDs to patients a week before going into surgery, because it cut down on the costs an average of $2000 per patient.[3] The patients were to listen to the CD prior to surgery to help them relax. Since we already understand the vast effects of stress on immune function, this should now make a lot of sense. These two examples are to show you just how powerful the mind is.

MBM will be one of the new frontiers in health care. Many of the therapies used in this field have been used for millennia in Eastern cultures, where they are more comfortable integrating spiritual and metaphysical practices into their care. Qi Gong, a Chinese meditative practice is commonplace in modern medical centers in China. It not only recognizes the importance of the breath, but also teaches that in order for health to exist, there must be proper flow of energy or Chi.[4] As we move further into the discussion of the mind, we will need to introduce more spiritual concepts. Through dance, for example, the body is able to experience the spirit, but through breath the mind is able to move the spirit. The ability to explore and express all of the components interchangeably is how we raise our consciousness.

What is Your Truth?

Currently, the randomized, double blind study is the gold standard in research. I know that currently this is the best tool we have to determine the effectiveness of a treatment, drug etc., however the whole point is to eliminate or mitigate all of the variables to pinpoint the specific effectiveness of what is being tested. In part the double blind study was introduced because the Placebo Effect was "skewing" the numbers. It seemed that prior to making the experiment "double blind" the expectation of something working was enough to create change in the body. Even if in reality the participant was given the control substance or inert substance. Even today, many doctors still use sugar pills in their practice because the expectation to get well creates enough of a benefit.

I spent a lot of time while I was at University really trying hard to understand the scientific method. I volunteered to be part of as many experiments as possible in a variety of fields, from Forestry, Psychology, Exercise Physiology, to Computer Integrative Systems. I wanted to understand how we decide what knowledge is? How do we decide what it is we are going to teach and pass on to the next generations? In a way, this is asking the question, what is truth? At the end of the day, we need people to study things in great detail. I applaud people who want to spend their whole lives studying a single topic in a field of study, but we need to realize that it has its shortcomings.

Especially when we take that information and apply it to individuals. We create labels that begin to define us and our actions. In real life, people are dynamic and all those variables that were factored out, either by way of method or statistics, can exist. And then when you add the greatest variable, which is the individual's ability to limit or deal with stressors, you truly hold a wild card. This is why it is so important to make yourself a partner in your health. Nobody will ever know you as well as you. Do your research, educate and have an advocate. But most importantly, learn to be present so you can access your own mind/body connection and listen to it.

Always remember that statistics do not tell your story. They are the story of a population. A great example of this right now is the debate over using the Body Mass Index (BMI) to measure obesity. BMI is a ratio that basically tells you if you are the right weight for your height. People, especially in the media, make all sorts of claims about body fat percentages and fitness, but it is a simple ratio. The reason it is used so much is that we have worldwide data all using this same measurement. We know as BMI goes up so does your risk for chronic disease. We have seen this positive correlation worldwide in all types of populations. Now, if you look at two people who are the same height and weight, but one is a couch potato and one is a trained athlete, you can simply tell by looking at them who is more healthy, active and fit, however they both could have a BMI that labels them as overweight. That is what I mean, statistics tell the story of a population. This becomes important when looking at the mind/body relationship.

If a trusted health professional tells you that you are sick, you will continue to direct your body to be sick. That isn't to say that there isn't healing to be done, but with that simple act, it limits your potential. Doctors know of treatment, statistics and experience, but they do not know your potential. Listen to the knowledgeable people around you, but make up your own mind on your own health status. There are many reasons why we need to give a diagnosis and prognosis, but take it with a grain of salt. Doctors don't see people because they are well, they see people because they are sick. That frames their experience of what is possible. It is your job to remember who you are, (and your potential) and what it is going to take for you to heal.

The Key Components of MBM

There are several principals common to MBM.[5] The first being that each person is unique. After the conversation we just had about truth and potential, I hope you can appreciate how important a concept this is. We tend to forget about our uniqueness and treat all patients based on a statistical probability that a specific treatment will cause more benefit than harm. But the cause and consequences of an illness will be different for each person simply because all aspects are interdependent and no one life is the same.

This leads us to another principal in MBM; that our bodies have an innate ability to heal. We discussed this in previous chapters, but I hope this is something that people will pick up and understand after reading this book. If we go back in history to when they developed Germ Theory, (which is still very integrated into our medical system today), we see how we got so far away from this truth. Germ Theory states that most diseases are a result of microorganisms. This led to the discovery of antibiotics and to improved methods of hygiene. These advances are remarkable, however it led us to believe that if we can kill the microorganism, we eradicate the disease.[6] The truth is that everyday we are exposed to all sorts of bacteria, viruses and fungi; the question to ask is why does one person get sick and another does not? If it were merely a matter of exposure, then wouldn't we all become ill? This type of thinking dominated as our pharmacology advanced. If we can isolate the causal factor of the symptom and suppress it, then we have success, but again this only looks at one part of a much larger picture. The ultimate cause of the flu is not simply exposure, because we all get exposed, but the body's inability to fight it off. Why is the body not in balance and able to self-correct?

Our current medical system needs to embrace and enhance the natural healing capabilities of the body and use it to our advantage. Otherwise, we are always swooping in after the fact. Prevention must be the focus. Treating only the symptoms is ludicrous, but in truth, our system does not allow for doctors to take the time to really get to know their patients. They are unable to get a picture of their lifestyle including: diet, exercise, stress, social support, environmental toxicities and mindset. Also, how many times have you lied to your doctor when they have asked you those questions? This is why self-care is important, so do your own self-analysis and figure out where you are out of balance. Look at it in terms of the optimal healing environment. Out of the five components, where should you focus your attention? Let the doctors do what they are trained to do and focus on your own self care – this is the partnership.

HEALING ENVIRONMENT

We do have capacity to heal ourselves, not always without help, but we can do more than we know. If our bodies are not in balance, including balance energetically, this ability will be stunted. We need to create the optimum environment for healing to occur. Putting a Band-Aid over the heart after a massive heart attack, will not work. We tend to do this figuratively with our health and even in the environment. Why did the heart attack occur? We look at the easy culprits such as saturated fat, cholesterol and maybe lack of exercise, but what about our relationships, vitamin and nutrient deficiencies, environmental toxicity, stressors, feelings of hopelessness, isolation and total lack of inner peace? Ask yourself, why is my heart breaking? There is no mistaking or coincidence, that heart related diseases are the number one killer in the Western world. Isolation and suppression of feeling are not only bad for our emotional and mental well-being, but also our physical heart. Our hearts are aching and breaking and all we want to do is put in a stint and get patients to take Statins. Statins, to their credit, are quite effective, but we need to take a step back and ask, why are we dying of heart conditions? Why do we keep making the choices that are killing us and yet will take whatever means necessary to stay alive? Now our body can rebound from all of those factors if the body has all the right building blocks. MBM gives us some of the best self-care tools, from relaxation techniques, to creating a positive mental outlook.

We rarely ever look at disease this way, but illness is a message. This is another key component in MBM. A common theme in this book, which I am hoping you are picking up, is that our bodies talk to us every day. They tell us when we are hungry, when we are tired, when we are overworked and even when we are ill. Some messages we are more aware of than others and with some we end up getting confused or misinterpreting. We need to listen and hear what they are saying and honor the message. Maybe it is a just a warning or a full blown wake-up call, either way it is a signal to you that there is work to be done. In working with the cancer survivorship population, many people say that they wanted to continue their lives just as they were living before diagnosis. They would drudge through the fatigue and the anxiety so to not 'give in' to the cancer. We are taught to fight cancer and even the term cancer survivor connotes a battle or a war waged. There are things wrong with this thinking.

First, to continue your life as is, is not hearing the message. It is not honoring your need for healing – to make whole. Our bodies get sick for many reasons and we need to explore those possibilities. Heed the message that our bodies are trying to tell us. If we feel tired then we need to rest. Fatigue and lack of rest tax an already burdened immune system. It is a time to feed your mind/body and spirit, to bring it in to balance, not to create further imbalance. Your bodies are going through such a time of upheaval you cannot continue to go on with business as usual. We have a hard time distinguishing between honoring our bodies and thinking that we are surrendering to the cancer or the illness. To give into your body is not to give up to the cancer. If illness is a message, then what is it saying? Surely, it is not that we should continue with the status quo. Why would doing the same things give us a different result?

Another key principal in MBM is to know and respect the energy field. We are going to talk about this in the later sections of the book, but it is important to mention it in this section as well. Our bodies have memories, in the mind, in the body and in the energy field. Balancing and clearing the energy field is crucial to maintaining good health. I really believe and hope that this too, will be one of the new frontiers in medicine. The body cannot find harmony or become whole without energetic balance. Our Western-based system wants to only look as far as the body, but that is as short sighted as only looking at genetics versus epigenetics. There is always the large and the small, the system and the cell, the whole and it parts to consider in our health. Without initially finding that balance, adding something to the system may work in the short term, but in the long term it is only adding to the disharmony of the system. Why we choose to do that over and over as humans is beyond me. We are constantly short sighted and always looking for the short-term solution. It has to stop, we need a better way.

Intention is another principal in MBM and a very important one. As we get further into the discussion of the energy field, this topic will be addressed more in depth, but it is necessary to mention intention when looking at MBM. Many of us move through life without setting an intention, sort of like a goal, but this agreement is made more on a spiritual and energetic level. Without a conscious awareness of our intention, we become bearers of unintended consequence. In don Miguel Ruiz's book, the Four Agreements[7], he discusses how we make agreements by the choices we make and our actions; we set an intention whether we know it or not. The aim in my mind, in mind/body interactions is to take the unconscious ideas and actions and make them conscious. To become aware of the programming we are running on. A great opportunity to do this is to follow your emotions.

Especially emotions like resentment, annoyance and anger. In those times, see your emotions as an opportunity for self-discovery and growth. Ask yourself, why do you feel annoyed? Where is that annoyance coming from, and what is it about you that is creating that emotion? Do not look to the other person for the answer, that emotion is an opportunity to make your conditioning conscious. Remember, emotions are pure impulses of energy, it is not until we interpret that emotion that it becomes something. The way we perceive that emotion is a matter of the mind and teaches us about our conditioning. Try it next time and you will learn a lot about yourself and your ingrained motivations. It is these connections that need to be made to overcome the ego.

Associations and Discernment

Dr. Rudolf Tanzi PhD, a professor of Neurology said that everything we encounter in our daily lives is judged based on our memories or associations. "We have fear, our memory of pain; we have desire based on our memory of pleasure".[8] These emotional responses interplay with our intellect and from that we see patterns of behavior emerge. We base our daily lives on these associations, many of which we created from a young age. For example, every time you are presented with broccoli, your mind will run through all the associations it has created around broccoli and from there you make a decision about whether to eat that broccoli or not. Most of this happens unconsciously and we are unaware of the specific times your mind referred to, to make this judgment. So imagine that one day when you were seven, you ate broccoli and threw-up afterwards. You were suffering at the time from a stomach flu, but your seven-year-old brain told your body that it was the broccoli's fault. From then on you have always disliked broccoli. Now as an adult, you maintain your dislike for it even though you don't remember that incident; somewhere in your subconscious you made that decision and you never challenged it, so that distaste for broccoli remains.

Our emotions are clues to these associations. The key is to become more aware of the associations we have created, and make more conscious decisions as to the best course of action. Many of these associations were created before we had a level of discernment. They were made as a young child and without question we still allow them to dictate our present actions. This can be stopped, all we need to do is to follow our emotions and open our hearts and minds to the possibility that we can choose differently. It is in the movement from moving the unconscious to the conscious that we can change our behaviors and rewire the workings of our brain. Nothing is static or determined; it only appears that way when we move through life without awareness. Once we gain this awareness in ourselves, we can begin to be more conscious of the choices that we make as a global community.

Chapter 10
The Wellness Identity

Part of understanding the mind/body complex is to have an awareness of who we are. What is at our essence? It is reaching this understanding that can have a profound effect on our health. We need this information to create our Wellness Identity. I use the term identity loosely, as the way we speak of identity is ultimately, an illusion. At the core of everything we are connected, and where I end and you begin is not as distinct as some would believe or would like. The boundaries and barriers between us are mind made - they simply do not exist. However, while this understanding satisfies a spiritual truth, we need to also understand it at the level of matter. So, for the sake of this chapter, and considering we are using the individual self as a catalyst and the source of change, we will discuss the Wellness Identity.

Our Identity, Our Health

How do we create (or more appropriately) remember our Wellness Identity? According to a study done by

Little et al[1], which looked at identity in the cancer survivorship population, identity includes the components of memory, embodiment and continuity. It is remembering all the qualities, characteristics, and virtues that make up who we are; it is our essence. In order to know that, it requires us to remember who we were before we got sick, not our roles or circumstances, but our essence. Sickness alters the way we see ourselves. It begins to limit our perceptions of who we are and what is possible. We get diagnosed and from then on we are given the label of dis-ease. As mentioned, even the term chronic illness is a long-term commitment to being ill. This changes the way we see ourselves and there are very real reasons for this. The illness itself may have changed the physiology, structure or function of the body in permanent ways. If you get a double mastectomy, that is a permanent change to the landscape of your body, but remember you are more than your body. Then there are many cases where some of the permanent changes are not as static as one might think. For example, if you were diagnosed with an arthritic joint, it would be wise not to determine your limitations from that label. Arthur Schopenhauer said, "Every man takes the limits of his own field of vision for the limits of the world." So it is important to remember what a dynamic being you are and not to allow labels to identify who you are. There is no doubt that there is a need to develop a new normal after a diagnosis, but it doesn't change what is at your essence. All of that remains regardless of the changes in the physical body. Remember what it means to be well, rather than perpetuate what is.

It has been said that during times of crisis' of health, it is easy for people to lose their sense of who they are or to say it another way, they lose their continuity of identity.

For example, maybe someone begins to identify themselves with the role of the patient or even worse as a victim. They begin to lose their continuity in the face of such extreme changes. People who fared better health wise are those who maintain secure anchor points to their essence.[2] This requires an integration of mind, body and spirit. For only then can people understand the essence of who they are. Once people begin to understand the mind/body interaction, they can see how much of their circumstance is exacerbated by treating the body alone. We need to remember who we were when we were well. To not only remember, but to know how that felt, looked, smelled, sounded and tasted. Remember also that wellness isn't just physical; it is emotional, mental, spiritual and energetic.

In that realm, cultivating our Wellness Identity, can aid us in regaining our health. Strength is gained by remembering what makes us strong, abundant and whole. We have bought into the idea that externalities, stuff and material gain makes us well and happy. Again, many of us have done this without conscious awareness by allowing advertising, socialization, roles, circumstance, material gain, labels and even intrusions of other people's energy fields to create our identities. Many of us wrongly identify ourselves with our jobs, our emotions or our circumstances instead of tuning into our essence. You might see how our misidentification with these things could lead us to confusion and bringing us once again into resistance of who we truly are. When we are only in touch with our bodies and mind as separate entities, (let alone no understanding of the interaction of the spirit) it is easier for us to integrate unhealthy and unnecessary determinants of identity into our perception of who we are. This limits our healing potential.

    I would suggest to everyone to do a vision collage to help them have awareness or maybe a reminder of who they are. On the vision board include pictures or phrases, anything that speaks to your identity. A note of caution, don't get too caught up in portraying your roles in life. You are not who you are because you are a lawyer. You may have certain characteristics that make you a great lawyer, which you may want to explore. For example, think of a person in your life that you love and admire. Do you admire them because of the role that they play i.e. Grandpa? Or does he possess qualities and strengths that make Grandpa special? That is a truer expression of essence than simply because he plays out the role of Grandpa. We all know that not every Grandfather is admirable just because of his title. It may also serve you to include things on your board that you know exist within you that have yet to manifest. Maybe you have always had a love of artistic expression, but you never pursued it. Create that as part of your Wellness Identity and then consider that maybe there is a physical manifestation from the suppression of that gift. A gift that you ignored because it didn't fit into the role you played.

    I ask people to do the vision collage in my cancer survivorship class and even though I explain every time not to over identify with the roles in their life, they inevitably show pictures of being a mother and a teacher etc. A good way to get around this is to remember yourself as a teen, or maybe even as a child and find the core of yourself that still exists today. Say in your adult life you are a teacher and you lose your job, which could be incredibly devastating if you put the entire stake of who you are into

The Healing Power of Belief

The Placebo Effect is really just a great example of the body's innate ability to heal. For a long time it was a thorn in the sides of researchers, which out of this frustration we birthed the gold standard of research, the randomized, double-blind study. In this type of research, there is random assignment and neither the researcher nor the patient knows if they are in the control group or the experimental group. It is said that 35% of people respond very well to placebos. Depending on what you are looking at, the range of the Placebo Effect can be anywhere between 0 and 80%. A 35% effectiveness rate is good, even for the best drugs.[3] The interesting part is why it works in the first place.

Think of your mind as the director, the one who tells all others what and when to act. If you have enough belief and expectation that a certain drug or process will work, the mind will direct the body to make the necessary changes, and healing begins. A few researchers even go as far to say that all healing that occurs is ultimately the result of this effect. Herbert Benson, one of the fathers of Mind/Body Medicine has tried to change the name of the Placebo Effect to "Remembered Wellness", due to it better describing how the effect works and the negative connotation that the Placebo Effect has.

He claims that in order for Remembered Wellness to work, three requirements must be satisfied. (1) Positive beliefs and expectations on the part of the patient; (2) Positive beliefs and expectations on the part of the health care professional; and (3) A good relationship between the two parties.[4] It is also important for the patient to see, feel and remember how the body functioned in its pre-illness state. Using visualization, affirmations and belief, the mind can direct the body to carry out the functions necessary to return to a state of health and wellness. This is why understanding mind/body interactions are so vitally important. If we understand how belief can change our biology in positive ways, we need to be aware of how the opposite is also true. Next time you are looking in the mirror and telling yourself how fat, ugly and worthless you are, think about what you are directing your mind to create in your body. It is worth a second thought, hopefully a conscious, positive one.

Your Vision Collage - Remembering Wellness

This is an exercise to remember who you really are; to connect with your strengths and your virtues. What are the qualities that define you or that you would like to define you? What makes you abundant? What are your stable anchor points of your identity? Find pictures from magazines, the Internet etc. and cut and paste them into a collage. Try not to get too caught up in depicting your roles; instead ask yourself what makes you good at those roles?

being a teacher. If you can identify what it is in yourself that made you such an exceptional teacher, you know that that is not lost even after the job is gone. Just as in illness. The illness may change your body and disrupt the day-to-day workings of your life for a period of time, but it does not change your core. That part of you exists eternally and it maybe even made your core stronger by adding a sense of self-efficacy to your already substantial list of virtues. These are the things you remember about yourself; these are the things you are to draw upon in the dark times.

Society's Labels

Ideally our ultimate goal should be the attainment of joy, purpose and inner peace. In a time of turmoil, inner peace may seem so far away, but when we forget what it is to have inner peace, we can only live in resistance. We put too much effort into the outcome, to survive instead of putting the time into what really matters, peace. Is your body up for a war or is it up for healing? It is a very different mindset and creates a different physiology. We are socialized in such a way, that there is no emphasis or even value in finding peace. Instead of placing importance on finding even a modicum of peace, we give people drugs that allow them to be numb, but let's not ever equate numbness to peace. The National Institute of Mental Health reports that about 18% of Americans suffer from Anxiety.[5] The rates of ADHD in children are steadily increasing and it is estimated that 60% of those children are being treated with drugs.[6] We need to be really careful with labeling our children. It changes the way they are treated and more importantly, the way they see themselves. This is again a Band-Aid solution. When will we start asking why more and more people are on anti-depressants or why anxiety is on the rise? Once again, we treat the symptoms and not the system. What is the root cause of this, individually and globally? I know that there is more than one root cause; some factors are environmental and some internal, but it would behoove us to explore what is at the root of this epidemic rather than look to mind altering medication. These children brains are still developing - this is uncharted territory. We are experimenting on our children and to put it any other way is a lie. They are still maturing emotionally, mentally and spiritually and we are denying them of the opportunity to get it right, to live their journey.

More and more we are drugging our children because they are not measuring up to our version of what we think is normal. We feed them crap, sit them in front of the TV and take away their physical activity and recess. We pack their day full of academic endeavors that doesn't bring balance to their highly creative and intuitive abilities. We see them as having too much imagination, too much movement and creativity, and we don't know what to do with them other than to medicate them. I am not saying that there aren't severe cases where people need medication, but we are overusing this option and disregarding all the non-invasive and more natural approaches. I just want people to realize that pharmacology is one approach, it is only one tool in the tool bag. It happens to be the approach physicians are primarily trained in, but it is still only one of many. It interferes with our essence, it disallows the nature of our true being. Some medications are absolutely life saving, but many are invasive and cause greater harm than good. Our goal should be to re-establish the balance in our body, open the channels of communication and to create the optimal healing environment. Most pharmacological approaches create further dis-ease in the body. Mind/Body Medicine provides us with many other tools in the tool bag.

You might be asking yourself, what does the drugging of our population have to do with the Wellness Identity? That is a good question. I mentioned earlier about being very careful with labels. We take these labels and use them to limit our possibilities. Again, look at the term chronic illness. What are we agreeing to when we take that label on? It distracts us from our real work, our journey towards the center of ourselves. The quest to understand and know the whole of ourselves. It is the gradual unfolding of our abilities and challenges that promotes spiritual growth. It is hard for us to know what is at our essence, when the challenges that were gifted to us are taken away or altered without doing the work.

Identity as a Measure of our Worth

Strip away all of those expectations, social norms and roles as we do not have to identify with them, they are a choice we make. Move from the heart space, your connection to all, and that will guide you to be well. Get help from health practitioners and do your own work – be that partner in your health. If your mindset is such that you ignore your own heart's truth, illness may follow. Part of our downfall, the greed that we have allowed to overcome us, comes from our misidentification. We have all heard the expression of 'keeping up with the Jones'. Is it not that drive, that misidentification with who we are and what's important, that led us into the worst economic recession since the Great Depression? People felt the urge to create false lives, allowing status or the illusion of status to drive our decisions. This isn't to say don't dare to dream, but instead to live the dream in the moment, live impeccably, not with material things but with integrity and resolve. What is your heart's dream? This is where we can fall prey to the ego mind, if we move unconsciously. Dreams should be derived from the heart when the mind is calm. We as individuals overextended ourselves to get stuff, and allowed predators to prey on that misconceived idea that stuff would bring us happiness. We could say that we, in the United States, have never been so consumed with consuming. Remember after 9/11, we were told to go out and start consuming again, to get back to business as usual. It will never be stuff that fulfills us. If that were true we would not be where we are. Caroline Myss, a brilliant mystic and medical intuitive, would say that all illness comes from us living out of congruence with our essence. This is the very nature of disease, this is the resistance.

In Buddhism, they speak of attachments and it is the attachments that cause suffering. Stop and think for a moment, what would happen if you were to let go of all of the attachments to outcomes, labels, status, and material gain? If those things were to no longer define you? If you got in touch with what is at your heart's center – your essence? If you spent time cultivating a relationship of awareness, honesty and impeccability with one's self? If you could be honest and proud about your own self worth without measurement against another's? This self-work leads to wellness and ultimately, inner peace. It is hard to even conceive of a world where this thinking can dominate, but I really feel that it will never be material gain that makes us better, happier or stronger. Even now if you think back to some of the best days of your life, does it ever have to do with money, status or the acquirement of stuff? The day I got married, and the birth of my son comes to my mind. Those days were not wonderful because of the extravagance, but because of their meaning. They were aligned with my true self. Being a wife and a mother are roles, that is true, but it is the meaning behind them rather than the roles themselves that brings me joy. The role has given me the opportunity to express and experience the greatest parts of who I am. Within all roles, emotions and circumstances there is the opportunity for the essence of who you are to be expressed, however if we don't look deeper into their meaning, we miss their importance in our healing. It is those virtues and characteristics that make us well and they are the strengths that we draw upon when we need to, not the roles. The challenges we experience in our life aid to strengthen us, not limit us. That is the mind's doing, but only if we let it. It is all about perspective.

Chapter 11

Gratitude and Transformation

We have so much to be grateful for. Our lives are filled with blessings even in some of the most dire of circumstances. Very often we choose not to see those gifts and those blessings because we refuse to live in the moment. We may fear that the good will be taken away, if we take the time to enjoy it and acknowledge it. It takes a level of awareness and acknowledgement to live in gratitude, and very often we lack both. The expression, "The grass always looks greener on the other side," is telling of our ability to look and live beyond the moment. To envy another's circumstance or position is to live outside of what is true in our own lives. A perfect example is the ridiculous importance we place on celebrities. We live in a virtual world of facades that we accept as truth. This separation is a tool for the illusion. Each individual has immense value, but none more than another. Again, if we can grasp our oneness then their accomplishments are our accomplishments. Not to be made possible without each and every one of us. Each of us has inherent value -

this again is not a call for a specific political agenda, as I am sure some will perceive it. Rather it is a universal agenda, a biological imperative for every living organism on earth to recognize our connectedness and also our individual gifts. It is out of cooperation that each one of our gifts gets the opportunity for expression. The giver and the taker require an agreement. Just as the smallest single celled organism has an effect on the entire food chain, so do our choices as an individual affect the whole. Gratitude is an expression of this understanding. Our natural world alone provides us with unlimited sources of gratitude. There is such perfection in the design, from the smallest organism to the most complex of systems. Nature is a great way to develop the habit of being grateful. This was discussed in the Holistic Fitness chapter.

Using Gratitude to Change Your Perceptions

Gratitude is a wonderful way to shift a perception of something. Wayne Dyer said, "If you change the way you look at things, the things you look at change". Gratitude can play a huge role in changing your perception of things you see negatively and helps to shift the energy that you have around a person or subject. Robert Emmons, who has spent many years researching gratitude, says it can allow us to "re-cognize" a negative event.[1] Using a grateful response to an unfortunate event can be a valuable adaptive tool, allowing the initial stress response to be mitigated. So it is one of those things, just like exercise and meditation, which affects more than one aspect of a person. It can calm the mind and the physiology of the body, but it also opens the heart. There are times when certain circumstances arise where you may be too overwhelmed to find opportunities for gratitude. In these instances you look beyond the circumstance to other areas of life where opportunities for gratitude exist. For example, right after diagnosis of a life threatening disease, it may not be an opportune time to see how this event is one you should be grateful for, but it will be a time to recognize all the other aspects of life that are worthy of gratitude. That is a common theme that I see working with people living with cancer; they are able to evaluate their lives and appreciate what is really important. In situations that are less alarming, it may be a perfect time to be appreciative of the specific circumstance. As in appraisal focused coping, it may allow you to feel better about the situation, lessening the impact of the stress response.

One tool that I find particularly effective, adapted from Ask and it is Given[2] is called the Rampage of Appreciation. This is simply to spend a few minutes going over all the things you have to be thankful for, from the most basic like being happy for the nice weather, to more stable life factors, such as your friends, family and work. I use this when I am in an unpleasant situation. For example, I was to teach a class and I hate being late for anything. It actually causes me quite a bit of stress and concern. On this particular day my husband was late getting home to watch our son and I only had a few minutes to get where I was going. It would be my regular reaction to stress out and curse my husband all the way to work, but that particular day I decided to use the Rampage of Appreciation. So on the way to class, I was thankful for my son, for my husband, for my job. It was hot that day, so I was thankful for my air conditioning, the beautiful weather etc. It turned out that every light on my way to class was green and I ended up getting there just on time. This, incidentally, helped a lot, but the best part was that when I got there I was calm, relaxed and in a wonderful mood, which is very conducive to teaching. Had I followed my already established pattern of stress and worry when under a time crunch, I would have arrived flustered and agitated. It may seem like a small thing, but the way we choose to engage in a situation plays a huge role in our stress levels. Please notice, once again my choice of words for they are deliberate. How do you choose to engage in situations? As mentioned, in times of stress or negative emotions, it is an opportune time to recognize your choices. Uncover how you operate and then make a conscious choice whether that serves you or if you deserve to choose better.

Being in the Moment

Gratitude also has a role in mindfulness. How can gratitude help us to live in the moment? Robert Emmons said, "Gratefulness is the knowing awareness that we are the recipients of goodness".[3] Again, it goes back to awareness. There is something important to understand, whether we are grateful for something of God's doing or another's doing, it involves interaction with others. By the simple act of realizing that there is something to be grateful for and expressing that appreciation - it is necessary to be mindful. Gratitude opens the heart and allows us to further share each other's spirit and gifts. Emmons said that the acknowledgement of goodness, is like saying, "Yes to one's life". Again, it is the resistance or the denial of one's true nature that prevents us from yelling "Yes" from the rooftops. But wouldn't it feel good to say yes? To live with meaning and conviction, to stop drifting through life feeling like you are at the mercy of everyone else and your circumstances. Stop, think and then say, "YES"!

Don't we all have that person in our life that always says no? That person that always thinks the worst is going to happen and then it usually does? The truth is that we program our brains, and our bodies to propagate that negativity. We in a way lube up those neural pathways, and then our minds will choose those preferred pathways over and over again. The first step to changing the behavior is to become aware of the patterns. We can't change what we don't know recognize. In a previous chapter, I mentioned that Cognitive Behavior Therapists believe that negative thinking can be the cause of depression.[4] I have heard many times from people who suffer from depression that they have a chemical imbalance. If we accept this as true then we should ask, why does the imbalance exist? You are not static - nothing about you remains in permanence. Only your mind can keep you there, by choosing the same things over and over again. If negative thinking can be a cause of depression, then what happens when we change the thinking? Going back to the first page of this section, how do we use our minds to direct our bodies to right that imbalance? Every time we have a thought, there is a chemical communication that accompanies that thought. When we have similar thoughts, for example negative ones, we send out similar chemical communicators. Candace Pert showed this in her research with neuropeptides. Neuropeptides are how nerve cells communicate with one another. In her research she found that other cells including those of the immune and limbic systems had receptor sites for neuropeptides.[5] This leads us to believe that our thoughts, immune function, our memories and stored associations are all interrelated. We are now learning that we can restructure our neural connections and opt for a more positive mental outlook thereby sending out different chemical messages to the body. We can change our bodies, our behaviors, and our thoughts as we move them into our conscious awareness. I want to be clear as we move onto the discussion about a positive mental outlook that here we are talking about the self talk that is going on constantly inside your head, not the appropriate emotional response to an unfortunate event such as a death of a loved one. In dealing with something like death, it is healthy to have and express feelings of sadness and depression for a time.

The Gift of Gratitude

(adapted from Watkins et al, study)[6]

So often in our lives we get caught up in our own stuff and give ourselves permission to over indulge in our own emotional state. Here is an exercise to release yourself of your own self-pity. Think of five people in your life that are struggling with something and need a hand-up. Write them a letter outlining all the things that they have done for you that you are grateful for. These could include things like helping you move, loaning you money or something less tangible like noticing you got your haircut when nobody else did.

This exercise helps you to expand your heart, hone your awareness skills and make a difference in someone else's life. We all want to be appreciated and sometimes it is the people who may be driving you crazy that are in most need of your appreciation. Once you have finished the letter, mail it to the person. You will brighten their day and maybe even help them to reframe their challenging situation.

The Attitude Needed for Gratitude

According to William Collinge, the important consideration in having a positive outlook is whether you suppress, repress or express.[7] A positive mental attitude comes from allowing all expression of emotion not just the happy ones. We have a hard time allowing ourselves to be sad or emotional. It seems we either deny them completely or identify with them so much that they become part of our identity. Neither option is optimal. Remember, it was discussed about letting emotions in and then letting them go. This isn't the same thing as giving up or giving in. Often the allowing of the emotions is seen as being weak, but I would suggest that it takes great strength to show weakness. In Taoist Philosophy, it is the weak that overcomes the strong. The strong may be hard as rock, but it is the water that runs over time that will overtake the rock, eroding the rock into sand. It is this cycle, from submission to domination, or this ebb and flow that is our natural state. So to deny the weak, we suppress the strong.

In a ground breaking study done by David Spiegel with Breast Cancer Patients, he found that women who talked about their fears of death in a group setting did better and lived twice as long as those that did not have the group support.[8] Until this study, the general consensus was that patients shouldn't talk about their fears because the emotional turmoil would worsen their illness, but in fact the evidence suggests otherwise. People who don't take their fears all the way to the end, have much more anxiety then those who face them. Resistance comes in many forms and disallowing the expression of a certain emotion that we consider undesirable, creates havoc on our systems energetically, physically, emotionally and mentally. We can expect better health outcomes from those who allow the full range of emotion, and who can maintain a positive mental outlook. An important component of a positive mental outlook is to have hope. Keep hope for yourself, but express your fears. They are not mutually exclusive, it is honest. When there is integrity in the system, we can achieve peace.

Chapter 12

Relaxation & Beyond

Herbert Benson in the seventies coined the phrase the Relaxation Response.[1] Basically it is when the body elicits a certain physiological response and allows the parasympathetic nervous system to initiate a chain of events. It is the opposite action of the fight or flight response discussed in Chapter Five. It is important to remember that balance is the key. The fight or flight response is not worse or better than the relaxation response - it is the counter balance. There are times when heightened arousal is necessary and it is equally important for times of relaxation. The illnesses result when one occurs far more frequently than the other.

As the body relaxes, we see a release of endorphins that cause a wide spread relaxation of the muscles which allows for better circulation because there is more space now between the cells of the body. This increased blood flow to the tissue allows for more oxygen to circulate, which in turn has an effect on the body's ability to absorb nutrients, build enzymes, release toxins and regulate hormone levels. This in turn creates an optimal environment for healthy cells to regenerate. Overall these homeostatic processes help to regulate the immune function of the body.[2] It is interesting to note that during meditation the body also decreases its metabolic rate. Don't worry though because this won't hinder your weight loss attempts, rather it is evidence of how quickly the nervous system can be calmed. This relaxation response is why most complementary medicine aims to reduce stress and promote relaxation. Many of us don't realize how beneficial it is for us to relax. I have just described to you the physiology behind relaxation, but I think that there are other benefits outside of the physiologic response.

What needs to happen before we elicit this relaxation response? First, we need to be mindful. Even if we are listening to a guided relaxation CD, our bodies don't automatically relax unless we begin to narrow our focus and quiet our minds. We need to be present and engaged in the moment. I personally feel that meditation is the best way to do this, but it is by no means the only way. When I first started doing Reiki, I quickly realized that although my clients would always reach a certain level of relaxation merely by way of the energy work, it didn't mean that their minds were still. Many people would come to a session after multiple cups of coffee and then race through traffic to get to the appointment. It would usually take them half the session to quiet their minds - if they were able to do it at all. At that time I was taking a Sport Psychology class at University and we were introduced to a progressive relaxation. I began incorporating a progressive relaxation technique using light as my source of relaxation. For example, "Imagine a beautiful white light moving down your face. With the warmth of the light and your breath you can begin to feel the muscles around your eyes release and relax". See the progressive relaxation script in the appendix.

I had great success with helping people to quiet their minds before we began the energy work. Stilling your mind can be a deeply spiritual practice (and I hope it is), but it also has very practical applications, as it is a skill that can be used in all aspects of life. Once we can learn to be mindful, our awareness of each other locally and global will expand. As Joseph Goldstein said, "Once we understand the process in ourselves, we understand the process in others". [3]

Meditation Basics

Meditation in principal is very basic, however to do it well takes a lot of practice. In this day and age, we take pride in our ability to multi task, to handle well all the daily demands that we have so artfully created for ourselves. In addition to all the demands, we have all sorts of environmental inputs, stimuli in our environments from computers, televisions, cell phones etc., that are not only putting out electromagnetic fields of their own, but also help us avoid solitude. Knowing now the vast response of the body to relaxation, how can we afford not to take this time for ourselves? A simple definition of meditation is the self-regulation of attention to a single point of reference. Now I am sure that anyone who has been to a Buddhist temple or an ashram in India will have a much more expansive definition that is more spiritual and eloquent, but to make my case from a quasi-medical perspective, this is the definition that I am going with. The truth is, that meditation has been explained and explored from many different perspectives in multiple religions. I would always encourage you, once you absorb basic meditation that you seek out ways to make your practice have greater meaning and depth by exploring it from a religious/spiritual vantage point.

There are two basic categories that meditation falls into, directive and non-directive. Directive meditation is when one focuses on an object or a process. This is where I would suggest that newcomers to meditation begin. This could be as simple as focusing on the breath, a word or a candle as the focus of the meditation. Again see the appendix for instructions on a basic meditation. Many people find it advantageous for them to have this anchor point in the beginning while they learn how to quiet their minds. Following the breath may be the easiest and will help most people avoid giving up too quickly. Monkey Mind or incessant self-talk has a way of interfering with even the best of intentions, and make no mistake, your mind will wander. Everyday will be different. There may be days where it is more difficult to calm the mind and on those days, just gently bring your awareness back to your anchor.

Non-directive meditation is the other major category. Jon Kabbat-Zinn, the director of an eight-week intensive program in mindfulness meditation, says that mindfulness meditation is, "Not so much about what you choose to focus on, but the quality of awareness that you bring to each moment".[4] In this style, the person would use directive meditation to create calmness and stability and then move to a state of allowing, where you allow thoughts to arise without judgment or attachment. It is a silent witnessing of the moment-to-moment thoughts that arise in the mind without editing or censoring. Although, this style of meditation may be harder in the beginning, it really allows for deep insights to be attained. Our body, mind and highest self may have some important information to tell us if we would just listen. I think that as we develop and nourish our abilities to listen intuitively to our bodies, to sit in solitude, we will gain insight into the greater truths of humanity.

One thing I want to mention, although we may have this preconceived notion of a mediator sitting cross-legged and still, the important thing is that our minds are still, not necessarily our bodies. Buddhists Monks have practiced walking mediations for centuries. Tai Chi is another great example of an active meditation. Any time you are in the present moment with a single point of reference, you are

---

Tips for Beginners

• Find a quiet spot where you can sit or lay down comfortably.

• Have a pencil and paper handy to write down any pressing information so it can be left for the moment, but not forgotten.

• If the mind wanders, acknowledge the thought, but gently push it aside.

• Do some light stretches before beginning.

• Focus on the breath to start or an affirmation/mantra.

• Continue to a sense of completion.

• Use a guided meditation CD in the beginning to get a feel for it.

being mindful. Meditation can happen while you are doing the dishes or going for a run. I think there is benefit to taking time out with a quiet mind and a quiet body. There should be a formal practice, but ideally you want to be able to take this skill on the road and incorporate it into your daily lives as much as possible. This would be considered informal practice. On the most basic level there is benefit to be gained by the body, but it also changes the mind and the way the brain functions.

Meditation & the Mind

Imagine your mind like a computer and in your conscious waking state you have many applications open on your desktop. These applications are of various activities in your daily life. We will call this the beta wave state. The brain is categorized into differing wave frequencies depending on the predominant oscillation patterns. Not all of the brain will be oscillating at the same frequency and different parts of the brain will present differently than others. For the sake of argument, we will call the waking conscious state the beta wave state. The beta wave state oscillates at a frequency of 15-30 cycles per second. The beta wave is the engaged and active mind. The alpha wave state has a frequency of 9-14 cycles per second and is characterized by a mindful, relaxed waking state. Theta waves occur during sleep, dreaming and in moments of deep meditative thought. They oscillate around 5-8 cycles per second. Delta waves occur during the deepest parts of the sleep cycle, also known as slow wave sleep, they oscillate at 1-4hz. It is interesting to note that many dementia related conditions, alcoholism, diabetes and depression, are correlated with a disruption of slow wave sleep[56]. Each state plays an important role in humanity as a whole. It is the whole that we are looking for even if we are not conscious of it. It is the void that we are trying to fill, the gap we are trying to close, and the force that we are trying to overcome. Stillness is the way to peace and fulfillment, the practice of meditation is but one answer.

When your desktop is full of open applications, it may be adaptive for multitasking, but for relaxation or sleep it is not. Have you ever had the experience of trying to read a book, only to realize at the end of the page that you didn't comprehend a word of it? We require that narrowing of focus or the self-regulation of attention to be on the words on the page rather than the thoughts in our head. In order to really create, comprehend or learn something novel, we need to close down all the applications that are running that do not pertain to the task at hand. We need to slow down those oscillations by narrowing our focus to whatever it is we want to accomplish. Studies have shown that meditation; especially non-directive meditation can increase attention and awareness by activating neural structures in the brain.[7] If we equate mental congestion to lack of ability to concentrate then we need to sort out the congestion by being in the present moment. How many things that take up space in our active desktop really need to be there? If we remove the mind made fears and anxieties, our attachments to emotions and the daily reminders that can be written down, we might find that we can run our lives and do our jobs more effectively and efficiently.

So many of us have trouble sleeping, and I hear things like "We cannot turn our minds off". It is like trying to go from 4th gear (beta wave state) to 1st gear (delta wave state) without gearing down. It won't work for a car and it doesn't work well for our minds and bodies. We all need to learn to gear down. How often do we work on the computer or watch TV right up until it is time to go to bed? All of that sensory input, (not to mention the effects of the electromagnetic fields being pumped into our bodies) and then we wonder why we can't get to sleep or can't stay asleep. Our minds need to gear down, just as our bodies do. Doing a progressive relaxation or meditation before sleep can aid us in doing this. Anytime we allow our bodies to relax, the better off we are at every level - mentally, emotionally, spiritually and energetic.

With meditation, not only are there the benefits to our bodies, but our mind's creative abilities can be more clear and effective. We can restructure neural pathways, create new associations to unwanted patterns and feel greater self-efficacy. "We don't solve problems with our breath, we dissolve them". Learning to release and relax every day, we can change our lives and the way we interact in our communities, our country and the world. There are health benefits on every level of our being. Our problems may not just simply disappear once we learn deep breathing, but if we look at the cellular impact of breathing we can see the starting point for change. Meditation is literally changing ourselves from the inside out. Having an influx of oxygen in our cells, causing that cascade of changes that helps us to live our lives in a more meaningful manner. How many of us function our best when we are sick and tired? How many of us have problems concentrating when we are filled with anxiety? These cellular changes affect our organ systems, which impacts every level of our bodies. Now we go out in the world and do our jobs with more vigor and clarity, and perhaps a more positive mental outlook. Just think how that affects the people that surround you. The more kind and pleasant you are to people, the more that spreads. If you fill your space, with health and a positive mental affect then it will be contagious.

So on one level relaxation creates the optimum healing environment by creating a calm and stable physiology in the body and a calm and stable mental outlook. Again, if we think of the mind as a tool for healing, a calm mind creates a calm body. In the next chapter, we will discuss how to take this relaxed state and altered state of consciousness to the next level to further our healing individually and globally.

Chapter 13

Meditation for Conscious Healing

In this chapter, I use the term meditation as a broad term that includes many altered states of consciousness. All of these states have several things in common: there is a decrease in oxygen, respiration, and heart rate and an increase in alpha waves in the brain.[1] These techniques can be used to treat many conditions from infertility, to high blood pressure to chronic pain. I have to mention that you would never make any changes to your current treatment without first consulting your physician, but they do work and can be an important part of your overall self care plan. Initially, the point is to create the relaxation response, but once that is mastered, you can aim toward targeted healing and insight (see figure on pg. 143). Is there a specific ailment that you want to target? Do you want to hear the words of your inner advisor? All of these things are possible when we move from a place of a calm mind and an open heart.

Figure 1. Meditation for Conscious Healing Pyramid

The Importance of Imagination

Our minds respond well to images and symbols. We can use this to our healing advantage. If we were to remember what it was like as a child to create whole new worlds with our imaginations, we can realize how powerful this can be. I really feel that these days, kids imaginations are stifled due to all the external stimuli from television, video games and computers. We revere our celebrities and sports figures, waste our time on the spectacle of reality television, and opt to put our attention on the external world, all the while thinking that we are somehow separate. The problem is that these images are being fed to us rather than being created from within. In that, we lose the knowledge of choice and allow others to create the illusion that they want us to see. It is our lack of imagination that perpetuates our short sightedness and it is our lack of stillness that creates disconnect. When we can no longer see beyond what is in front of us, then the world can seem hopeless. We will perpetuate the viscous cycle of repeating what we see, because we are unable to see that there are other options. When we should be in awe of the limitless possibilities of the human mind and moreover, the human spirit. We just need to plug into one another and truly all the information is right at our fingertips (more on that later).

If we can take back our imaginations, we can find our way out of many of our health problems and universal conundrums. We need to believe and perceive that all things are possible. The techniques and modalities described in this chapter harness the power of our imaginations. They speak in the language and the symbols that our mind understands. That is what targeted healing is all about, using our imaginations to our advantage.

Targeted Healing

I had a woman in one of my classes that would use visualization during her radiation treatments. She would imagine a circle of white light creating a barrier between the tumor and the healthy surrounding tissue. She imagined that this barrier would only allow the radiation to target the tumor and leave the healthy tissue untouched. This is a great example of targeted healing. I use targeted healing when I experience headaches. I lie down and find my center and begin to follow my breath. Then I imagine the blood vessels in my head vasodilating or expanding and allowing the blood to flow easily and freely through the vessels. Now, is it necessary that I know how blood vessels dilate? Not really. If we think of our mind as a director and more over as a tool, by just having that thought, the mind is directing the body to accomplish the desired task. You don't need to be a Physiology major, all you need is to be mindful and set the intention for an outcome to occur.

Guided Imagery (GI) is another example of how we can use our imaginations to create targeted healing. Dr. Martin Rossman, describes GI as an applied form of mediation that uses intention, attention and imagination.[2] Guided imagery can be used in so many ways, once the skill of being present is mastered, you can further the healing by using images, sounds, sights and colors, for example. Some people really resonate with nature, and a nature visualization can bring relaxation to some people that is unparalleled in a simple meditation. Guided Imagery is not only about being fed images, though that is a great way to ease into the process, but in the end it is about allowing free flowing communication between our bodies and our minds. Guided Imagery can be a great way to gain insight as well. One of my favorite techniques to do is to take people to meet their inner advisor. Many practitioners have their own version of this technique. Having a person talk to their inner advisor can give them insight to their illness, what they need to do or possibly suggest the best course of treatment.

Hypnotherapy is a great tool for the mind, helping to shift those negative thought patterns. To change established associations that may exist just underneath our conscious awareness. These associations, whether conscious or not have an effect on the functioning of the body. A person who is in hypnosis reaches a meditative like state. Very often they are induced into a hypnotic state via eliciting the Relaxation Response. Meditation and hypnosis are both altered states of consciousness with a narrowing of focus, however in hypnosis, you have heightened suggestibility which allows you to actively vent or work on a specific issue.[3] The intention of the session and the goals are clearly defined at the outset and a person works on changing unwanted behaviors or seeking specific outcomes. Many people are put off by hypnosis because they have seen too many stage acts and think that they will be at the mercy of the hypnotist or hypnotherapist, however we enter hypnosis all the time without knowing it. Have you ever had the experience of driving down the highway when you suddenly realize that you do not remember the last stretch of highway? That is a form of environmental hypnosis. You are in an altered state of consciousness, where you have disassociated from what is going on in the external environment and have put your attention to the thoughts in your head. It is this ability to disengage from the less useful aspects and zone in on others that allow the person to create new associations and thought patterns.

Most people know that they would like to elicit change on a conscious level. If you were to take smoking for example, many people in their conscious waking state could find many reasons to quit. It makes them smell bad, they waste too much money, they have decreased levels of energy etc. Now for all the good intentions they have consciously, there is also a drive from the subconscious brain to maintain status quo. The subconscious has the ability to derail and sabotage the conscious mind's best intentions. The thing is that through hypnotherapy, you can gain access to the subconscious mind to re-create the established associations. You can alter that drive toward smoking so that there is a congruency between the conscious and subconscious mind. In hypnosis you are able to bypass the critical mind; that is the mind that reflects, judges and self deprecates by way of a hypnotic induction.[4]

An induction is the process of accessing the subconscious mind. Hypnotherapists have various methods for this. Once the appropriate depth of hypnosis is achieved, and this is dependent on the type of issue you are working on, you can begin to create new associations in the mind. Now, it is my opinion that it is easier to do some of this work with the help of a hypnotherapist, but not necessary, if you are able to achieve a level of mindfulness. We cannot forget that we have a great affinity for self-healing. We are not encouraged to look at it that way, but if you can create the optimal healing environment, the body can achieve amazing things. Be aware of when you need to get outside help, but do not discount your power and your abilities.

Self-hypnosis is a great tool for many people and a good example of targeted healing. Though self-hypnosis is more of a conditioned response, the effects can be just as positive. Self-hypnosis is a state of focused attention brought about by the individual through repetition of a relaxation exercise. Once the individual is in this state, the person makes self-suggestions. These suggestions help to change unwanted thought patterns or behaviors. This can be an incredibly powerful self-help tool that not only brings about relaxation to the body, but also shifts the mind. The best time to create change is to do self-hypnosis right before bed. This allows the suggestions to more readily slip into the subconscious mind as the person drifts off into sleep.[5]

Biofeedback is also a tool for targeted healing. In biofeedback, the individual is using his/her mind to control functions of the body, which are normally under involuntary control. This is the outcome of many mind-body measures, but in the case of biofeedback, it is means as well. Initially the individual uses feedback from various pieces of equipment that measures all types of physiological processes. This could be something that measures blood flow, respiratory rate and electrical activity of the muscles, brain and heart to name a few.[6] The type of feedback that they receive is dependent on the type of equipment used and what health issue they are working on. Once the skill is mastered, the individual would hope to be able to replicate the outcomes without feedback from the equipment. Again, it requires the self-regulation of attention and mindfulness. If the individual does not put all of his/her focus towards achieving the goal, they would not be able to elicit the desired response. This is a great example of the mind/body connection and hopefully where health care is headed.

During the waking state, affirmations can be used also to shift thought patterns. Affirmations and mantras are sometimes used synonymously, but that is not always correct. Affirmations are phrases used in the present tense to establish or reaffirm positive character traits or behaviors.[7] A Mantra can be a phrase, but traditionally is a sacred sound or group of sounds that have deep healing properties. Thoughts have energy, prayers have energy, words and sounds all have energy and by energy, I mean a vibrational frequency. Using a repetitive sound or phrase can help to realign the body and mind. From a purely psychological standpoint, the use of a repetitive phrase can elicit change in thinking, but from an energetic standpoint, it changes your vibrational frequency (I will explain this in detail in the next section). When I teach classes on meditation, I love it when I have a group willing to chant

OM with me. I just want them to experience how that sound (sounds more like Aum) feels as it resonates with their bodies. It is an amazing feeling, having it move through your body, and bringing alignment to the body, mind and spirit. It is rare though for me to have a class where people are open to chanting. We are not accustomed to doing that in front of others. While I believe that there are healing properties when it is done solo, I thinking there are added benefits to doing it as a group. I have been at conferences where a room of hundreds of people chant OM in unison and the experience is unparalleled.

Mandalas are the perfect example of how the mind, symbols and vibration intermingle. Mandalas are the perfect representation of the journey from the macrocosm to the microcosm. We most associate mandalas with the Buddhist and Hindu traditions, sometimes being called Yantras, however these beautiful concentric shapes can be seen in all traditions, even Christianity. They help us to understand our connectedness by moving us inward; the synthesis of the outer external world and the inner world of the individual. Carl Jung said, "I realized more and more clearly that the mandala is the center; it is the expression of all life; it is the path of individuation." Once we become whole with ourselves, we can understand the larger whole. This is our holographic nature. These sacred geometric shapes have healing properties that align the mind and the body on a level we may not be conscious of. Mandalas can be used in various ways. You can use a mandala for meditation, either as the focus of the meditation or as the inductor of a meditative state. The mandala is represented by the circle, showing that there is no beginning and no end. In much of life, the path to experience is through understanding the dichotomies. We live in a system of polarity. Being able to conceive something relative to something else allows you to know what your beliefs are, your strengths and weaknesses, etc. Mandalas represent the complete, the whole of us as individuals and the entirety of the universe. They have the ability to teach us the utmost truths of existence. I would like to see them become tools used in hospital settings and as a personal tool for self-transformation.

Why would these skills/therapies be advantageous to us as a growing population? If we can teach biofeedback, self-hypnosis or affirmations etc. to the masses it could greatly reduce our dependence on pharmacological approaches. Drugs play an important role, but there are some areas where conventional Western medicine falls short. Again, our system needs to become more integrative and there are many reasons for this. (1) These skills are only mastered once a level of mindfulness can be achieved. A more mindful population breeds compassion and connectedness. (2) If we were to adopt this mode of thinking, then we can teach people to help one another heal themselves, rather then be at the mercy of our health care system. (3) Reiterates how important the mind/body relationship really is - as we become conscious, the world becomes conscious.

Insight: Listening to Your Highest Self & The Connection to the Whole

Insight is the most valuable tool we have and it is a bi-product of creating a calm mind. We have wisdom and knowledge available to us beyond our current comprehension. This is how we connect to God and to each other. It is also in these moments that we experience

HEALING ENVIRONMENT

our oneness. We are all connected, meditation develops our awareness of this connection. Non-directive meditation lends itself to insight, but there are also visualizations that can be done to help you get in touch with your inner wisdom. I went and saw a hypnotherapist to help me understand my barriers to prosperity. The extent of the session was a guided visualization that allowed my subconscious mind to speak to my conscious mind through the use of symbols. The information that I gleaned from the experience was invaluable to me and I am still uncovering all the messages.

One of my favorite tools that I teach clients is to help them create their own Place of Power. I borrowed that term Place of Power from Carlos Castaneda's book, Journey to Ixtlan[8] (see Place of Power in the appendix). The point of this exercise is to help clients create a healing sanctuary that they can go to knowing that it is a place of deep healing, insight and centeredness. The more this exercise is practiced, the more powerful it becomes. Once this exercise is mastered, you can invite people into your Place of Power that may have wisdom for you about a particular issue or illness. Very often this is best done with a practitioner, but the Place of Power is something that can be done at home for self-healing.

I can't tell you how many times I have found answers in my meditations. This book came to me in a meditation. This is not an active process where I am thinking about what needs to be done. I set an intention before I begin and then I start my belly breathing. Then the stillness sets in, my mind is calm and my heart is open. It is in this space that I hear the wisdom. Then as I finish my meditation, I sit in gratitude for the opportunity to remember that everything I need to know, already is. Sometimes it is a matter of reframing and sometimes, I understand things with a different level of awareness. Then there are times when all that happened is mild relaxation and centeredness. Not every meditation is still, sometimes it is a work in progress. So don't be discouraged, every day is different and it takes practice. This is not something we currently value and so it goes against the current ways of our culture. This is not the moment to multi task - to work on enlightenment and the grocery list at the same time. It is to bring the body, mind and spirit back into alignment. All the information that the soul needs is available in the right frequency. Imagine you are tuning a dial on the radio, it is in this space that love flows and all things can be remembered.

So the Matter of the Mind

From a purely health standpoint, there is benefit to making stress reduction and relaxation part of your everyday regime. It has so many physiological benefits that even if you do not want to glean the awareness that the practices and therapies have to offer, it still needs to be part of the prescription for good health and specifically necessary as part of the treatment of chronic illness. Now to further the discussion, learning to be present has very practical benefits, in your everyday life. Whether you are trying to learn something novel, comprehend something very important, enhance creativity and increase productivity, the skill of being present has limitless benefits. But as always, let's take it even further. We are spiritual beings. We need to grasp this concept very quickly because our technology has far surpassed our ability and understanding of connectedness. This is destroying our health and our planet. In the end, it will be our technology, innovation and ingenuity that will bring our new paradigm into fruition, but only when our spirituality has evolved as well. Science without spirituality will lead to our destruction.

Therapies such as meditation, guided visualization, hypnosis, use of mandalas and mantras help us journey inwards. They evoke the Relaxation Response, then as you deepen your practice with whatever mind/body modality resonates with you, you have access to targeted healing and insight. It is the insight and the understanding of our oneness that will help to change the world. The ability to be present and mindful gives us the opportunity to know the truths of our bodies, nature, and all of existence. Find which therapy or therapies resonate with you and use them daily. Not only for your health, but also for your spiritual growth. These modalities also help us to understand the energy field that exists around each and every one of us. This is also part of our healing process as humans. The body and the mind requires acknowledgement of our spirit for good health. The earth depends on us to recognize this and the tools given to you in this section will help you know this truth.

Part IV

Transcending Our Limits

Chapter 14

Use the Force:

Understanding Consciousness

On one level it is true to say that all healing is self-healing, but it goes much deeper than that, as all healing is ultimately spiritual healing too. It requires us to engage in the part of us that is connected to the all. Beyond the ego, beyond the mind and far beyond the body, to the part of us that is connected to Source. It is not our place to ask why something has happened and then look to God or the Universe for the answers. The answers always lie within. Still many people may ask, "Why would God do this to me?" That question is a matter of the mind, of the ego. Just as we must do the physical work, we must also do the spiritual work – the soul level work at the center point of our being. This is a timeless space, where logic and reason are not contemplated, there are no deductions to be made, and where diagnostics are not of concern; it is beyond all that. Our diagnosis is a label for a manifestation whose origin started well before its appearance in the physical body. You may ask, "Then why do some people get well, when they have no idea of the soul or Source"? First, I would remind you that healing is becoming whole, which is why, as spiritual beings we need to engage our spirit in the process. Curing is a medical term that means the end of an illness. They are not the same, even though they are often used as such. We all have the power to get well, and even when the ego self doesn't understand how or why, that part of us that connects to the Source, knows better. There is a part of you that still remembers who you are and what you need to learn. Upon our arrival on this earthly plane we volunteer to enroll in earth school and the lesson plan is decided upon before our incarnation here on earth.

Our Earth Lesson

We are the Universe trying to know itself. But does knowing itself mean we have to do it dichotomously? Can we know wholeness, instead of separation? Can we work together, instead of creating disparity? Can we maintain individuation while understanding universal entirety? Maybe the only way we understood our lives was to experience the opposites, but what if that becomes no longer necessary? What if we establish stability in the ego, and expand our awareness so that it no longer requires us to explore the either - or, but envelope the all?

We chose to live this life of polarity and it served us. We created difference when there wasn't any in order to experience ourselves. This has driven our cultures, our technology and our understanding of the world, but I believe we are being called to do more. What if it is time to move on to our next lesson? To move past this and to move to a place of cooperation and not competition? Competition has propelled our civilization in amazing ways, but it is an old paradigm and we are ripe for a shift. This is why our health is beginning to fail on a mass scale, because it is resistant to the required change. We have a driving force within us to re-join the whole and we are ignoring it.

Describing the Indescribable

Where does our spirit reside? Does the understanding of spirit require us to have faith in God? I have spent a lot of time incorporating the words spirit, consciousness, energy and vibrational frequency into the other sections, but what do they all mean? These terms are not perfect, nor do they conjure up the same idea in everyone reading them, but it is necessary we understand the energetic underpinnings in order to understand their role in our health and healing.

There is a unifying force that governs all things. This is the field of consciousness. All the information, light and energy is contained within this field. As humans we have our own energy field that interacts with the larger field of consciousness. Through our hearts we connect to this field, where all of our energies intermingle and co-create. Our heart is our first point of contact with this field of consciousness. At this point every thing is still pure impulses of energy. As our mind receives this information and interprets it, the information becomes transformed and transmuted into much denser energy states. Our mind/body creates an emotional and biochemical response to the interpretation. It becomes a feedback loop that seemingly happens simultaneously. We are constantly exchanging light and information between one another. This is the easiest way for me to conceptualize our oneness. And our collective interpretation of it becomes our collective consciousness. This is why it is relative to the masses. When this energy, light and information transfer and interpretation happens without conscious awareness, we create unintended consequences. We also derive truth from our limited, unconscious and subjective experience of the field. Our fear, conditioning and socialization distorts our interpretation of it.

At its source however, there is only pure energy that is moved through the matrix. This is my energetic understanding of God. So on one level we are all God, but there is an aspect of God that is greater than all of us. This is the underlying force that encompasses all that is, ever was and ever will be. So essentially we are all part of the creating and all part of the destruction. Each of us has responsibility for both the good and evil, but collectively we are the decision makers. We just haven't been conscious of it. Consciousness is the creative force in the Universe, it is through this that matter is created. This is the true basis of free will. I feel that we can all experience Spirit moving through us if we pay attention. And once we can do that, we can have access to all knowledge and can harness our limitless potential.

Using the Force

Energy Medicine for this reason must be one of the components of the optimal healing environment and part of health care. I volunteer my time as a community education teacher and one of the classes I teach is on Understanding Your Energy Field. I love teaching this class because I get the opportunity to introduce people to this way of thinking. Also, when I get the opportunity to give healing sessions to people who have never experienced it before, they begin to contemplate the unknown. It gets them thinking about deeper spiritual truths and energetics, even if that isn't the words they use. They get to experience something that they never thought existed, or existed only intellectually for them. I believe it is the Holy Spirit that is running through them. It is the life force that governs all things. Our personal energy fields are our expression of our life force, a smaller, denser part of the greater force of God, Source or Spirit.

In a much denser state, we have all experienced this field, even without conscious acknowledgement of it. Have you ever walked into a room and could tell the feeling of it? Whether it was good or bad? Or met someone and right away were drawn to them or repelled by them even though you don't have any reason for it? Many of us might chalk it up to their appearance either attracting you or turning you off, but it is more than that. You experience their field and we pick up on that, which is part of the larger field of consciousness. All things have energy, so it is no coincidence that we use EEG, EMG and EKGs to measure the electrical activity of the brain, muscles and heart. If we can measure the vibration of a single muscle fiber, is it such a stretch to imagine that all the muscle fibers together would create an electrical field? And that those fibers form a muscle and that muscle has a vibration? And all of the muscles and organs together create a larger unified vibration and so on. We are energetic beings, even if science hasn't fully found a way to measure it. Once you practice working with the energy field, it becomes not only plausible, but downright tangible.

Part of the problem is that many of us don't know how we best experience this field. Some of us who are visual can actually see the field and the energy systems. Others of us can feel it, sense it or even hear it. The first hurdle in experiencing it, is knowing how to engage with it. The way that it flows is a determinant of our health and ability for healing. Acupuncture works on the premise that the proper flowing of Chi will allow for good health. Many different energy systems exist within the body, but regardless of the modality that you are coming from, the energy is the same. It is the energy of the all, the divine of God. This is where our intuition is derived from. Intuition comes from our ability to follow our breath, ground ourselves in the present and open our hearts to this field. Caroline Myss, a medical intuitive whom I respect so much, explains intuition in a fascinating way. Intuition in itself is not spirituality, it is a tool one can use to glean insight. It is the ability to tap into the field of consciousness and then what you choose to do with that knowledge then can become part of your spiritual journey.[1]

So many obstacles to our health would be overcome, if we understood this field. We would be able to make great leaps in self-healing. It would have an immediate impact on how we treat others, promoting respect and tolerance among people of other religions and races. One of the first things I began to notice when I started doing Reiki was how quickly and easily my compassion grew. People who on the outset I judged for whatever reasons, became quickly an object of love and acceptance. It becomes rather impossible to hate or fear someone once you experience them energetically with the intent of healing. The feeling of oneness is overwhelming at first, then incredibly comforting. There are moments when I am working within someone's heart chakra that all I can feel is an abundance of gratitude for being able to share so deeply and intimately with someone. To really experience non-romantic or universal love for another person with whom you have no previous relationship with, is a moment worthy of gratitude of the highest order.

The Degradation of the Field

Another consequence in experiencing the field is appreciating our connection to the earth. Plants communicate with each other, animals communicate with each other and whether we know it or not, they all communicate with us through this field. I have heard the argument made that God put the animals here for us, but when you look at how we treat the earth and the animals, do you think that is what She intended? For the animals to be treated more like a process than a living thing? We have mechanized the system to the point of inhumanity. All of life is part of the field, when we degrade one aspect, we degrade ourselves. Stop and contemplate our health, the plants, animals and our earth as part of a larger energetic matrix. A matrix that intimately connects everyone of us. Hold that thought for a moment in your heart center, what are we doing with that life force? What are we creating or more appropriately, destroying?

I remember many years ago I met a hunter (Back then, I was on my high horse and was totally disgusted with the idea of someone being able to shoot another animal). This man was very blunt with me and explained that every time he kills an animal there is always a moment where he thanks God and the animal for the sacrifice of his life to feed his family. Can you say that when you pick out a steak at the grocery store? The hunter knew what it was like to take a life and showed gratitude and reverence, for he knew and appreciated the impact that that life had. How many of us think twice about the life of the chicken or the pig when we grab the package out of the fridge? This does not mean we should never eat meat again, but appreciate the connection we have to our food energetically. How is the consciousness of that food passed on to us if it was treated inhumanely and unsustainably? Again, whether it is a fellow human or animals, any degradation to the field is degradation to ourselves.

I have heard the argument made many times that it doesn't matter what we do here in the West, we are still going to have enemies that want to kill us or people on the other side of the world using more energy and resources. That argument is one of a child and it is time to mature. Each one of us needs to do what we can do. We need to move from our own center point and move outward. The shift begins in each one of our hearts and moves out to our families, to our community, to our nation and beyond. Energetically, if we change, we can create change in others. Not through force, but ultimately through love. Whether we are consciously aware of it or not, we affect others through our actions and through our energy. Change the energy, change the action. If the world's patrons sought out inner peace would we still have the motivations to kill, maim and rape? Would we still have the impetus to rape the earth of her resources that took millions of years to develop and mature? Always hold the words in your heart center and seek to know if they are true. That is all I can ask.

Coming Together

The point of energy therapy is to assess the health of the energy field or aura and to assess the energy centers. I always feel uncomfortable using the word aura. I know for a long time that science and New Age Philosophy were incompatible with one another in mainstream academia. Many still see it that way. However, whether you want to call it an aura, an energy field or our biofield, it is all semantics. Each one of us needs to get comfortable with whatever term they wish, but we must know it. All of us need to come from our own perspectives when it comes to understanding the energy of our own bodies and our collective field of consciousness. As with all things, there are many levels of understanding to be explored and the world must come together, each in their respective fields to create a universal contemplation. I feel energy, but I don't understand the mathematics or physics of it. So much of my understanding comes from my intuition, from visions during meditations, dreams and during energy work with myself and others. Others will be able to explain it through numbers and calculations, and some through myth, but do not dismiss others expression of it as wrong. Our contemplation is oneness; this is the unification of the left and right brain, the Yin and the Yang, the mind and the body. The movement from competition to cooperation.

It is our nature to be skeptical and that has proven to be productive and creative, but when it is attached to chronic cynicism, and unconscious interactions, we lose all ability toward wonderment. We stifle our imaginations. The ability, and the all important opportunity to see things in a completely different way. In science we make small increments of improvements, one built upon the other. What I am suggesting is to jump right out of the ballpark. Through our ability to look inward and understand that connection, we can make a conscious universal choice to choose something better. We all need to tap into our right brain. I am speaking somewhat figuratively from a psychosocial perspective. Our brains do not have a simple, clear-cut overarching hemispheric function, but we can use this model for the purposes of learning. In academia, we largely value logic, analysis and regurgitation of facts. There is no emphasis on intuition, compassion or wisdom. We don't teach people how to engage in the field of consciousness. Jill Bolte Taylor, a brain scientist, had the unique opportunity to explore both sides of her own brain while having a stroke.[2] She gives a fascinating talk recounting the thought processes she experienced in that moment. She explains how the right side of her brain was all about the now, about our oneness and at the same time, her left side was logical, calculating and expressing concern over herself as an individual. The take home message from her speech was that if we could all spend more time in the right side of our brain, the world would be a much more loving, compassionate and mystical place. Can you imagine if God or Spirit was more than an intellectual understanding? If we could feel Her moving through us and make the connection that we are connected to all of life? There are infinite amounts of possibilities once we learn to tap into the more abstract ideas, the greater contemplations. Our energies as a whole create and destroy. In order to create something better, we each need as individuals to understand how it operates, how it affects our health and how through it we can change the world.

I am not about dismissing science. I just think we need to put an equal amount of time and attention into developing ourselves as multi-sensory beings. We need to place value on intuition and how to use our emotions to understand and dismantle our programming. Think about the gains we could make if these two sides were equally matched? Right now, we overvalue this all or none response. "Well, if my way is good, your way must be bad. If drugs work then let's devalue all other natural tools we may have". This thinking is getting us into trouble with our health, our environment, and not to mention, geopolitically. Once we see our world energetically, we no longer need dichotomous ways to understand it. We will understand we are a holograph of a larger whole.

Chapter 15

The Energy Matrix: Healing the Spirit Within

A case could have been made to begin this book with this section as everything we know streams from the field of consciousness or our energy fields. It is the basis for everyone, and everything. While in the previous chapter, I talked about our energy fields as an extension of God and Universal consciousness, we can also explore our energy fields from the perspective of self healing. Just as with meditation, it can be a spiritual practice, but it can also be used for basic relaxation. These are spiritual truths with practical applications. However, when you go to your doctor's office today, the energy field will not be mentioned. The reason being that we have yet to invent an instrument capable of detecting it, that mainstream science approves of. Due to our reliance on inferring truth from the scientific method, we don't value what we cannot measure or what doesn't seem to fit into our current paradigm. However, the vastness of anecdotal evidence for energy fields has brought Energy Medicine into our hospitals anyways. There are now Healing Touch Practitioners on staff in some hospitals around the country.[1] There is a widespread movement around the world to bring Healing Touch to every nurse, but why, if there is little researched-based evidence to support the claim?

Though the energy field may not be part of modern medicine, it sure has been a part of human existence. Whether you want to call it Chi, Prana, or the Holy Spirit is up to you, but we can all sense it is there, if we pay attention. As mentioned, the proper flow of Chi is a major tenant of Eastern medicine. The use of laying on of hands has been around for over 2500 years and probably even longer. It was even said that Jesus healed people with the laying on of his hands in the Bible.

The Premise Behind Energy Medicine

Illness starts in the energy field and moves inward. There are seven layers in the aura or energy field and all things are felt in the furthest most part of the field.[2] The physical layer and the physical manifestations are the last to develop. This adds a whole new dimension to mind/body interactions and truly makes the case to incorporate the spirit into healing. The reason that Western medicine isn't overly successful is that it treats symptoms once they manifest on the physical plane. More than likely, there are emotional and/or mental factors at play and these factors also have an energetic representation in the energy field. When those aren't addressed, neither is the real issue or the root cause of the problem. We are just treating the physical manifestation or the symptom and not the emotional or mental cause.

Mind/body interactions are truly more impactful when we fully understand the energy field.

Breath and mindfulness can heal the world, because it allows us to experience the field of consciousness and connect to our oneness. I know that this idea will be criticized for being too simplistic, but in all fairness we have not tried it. Whether you are speaking about thoughts, emotions, or food – it all affects our consciousness. Different vibrations can heal or harm us and everything has a vibration. This is common knowledge in the medical world, especially in Physical Therapy, though not from a metaphysical perspective. Have you ever seen where a Physical Therapist will put the electrical currents on a person to treat an injury. This is because they know that certain types of cells heal better or regenerate faster using certain frequencies. That is because all things vibrate and all things are energy. Even our thoughts put out a vibration, which is why **MBM** has such huge opportunity moving forward. They send energy out into the universe and the universe responds to its creative force.

Images, sounds, smells and intention all have a vibration. How do we integrate these things into our calm and relaxed bodies to intensify healing? So much of our physical pain and suffering comes from stagnant or stuck energy in the body, it is important to move that energy out of the body. This is where mind/body interactions and energy medicine marry. In this, it is important to make things tangible. In fact, the more we make some of the intangible, tangible to our mind - the more compliant we can make the body. For example, if we give pain a shape, color, size and location, we can then learn to modulate the pain. We can use visualization to change the shape and size of the pain, thereby symbolically lowering the intensity. Also, we can symbolically surrender and release anxiety in the same way. If we give the anxiety tangible qualities, it makes it easier for us to release it. How does the anxiety look and feel? What material is it made of? If we can identify it in this manner, we can aid the healing through visualization. The same premise works in journaling for example. If you give your feeling words then the words can be released from the body in the form of writing.

All of these visualizations also have energy behind it. Any time we set an intention to create healing, we make an energetic agreement. Our intention is a spiritual contract that shifts our vibrational frequency to match the desire. If we can hold that intention for long enough we have the opportunity to manifest on the material plane. So our thoughts hold the power of creation on every level. They change our physiology, our emotional response and our energetic frequency.

If again we go back to the resistance theme, the communication and information we are receiving from our own energy field and those around us is being ignored, denied or misinterpreted. The information is vital to our healing. All it takes is for us is to move inwards with a calm mind and an open heart. We are vibrational beings - organs and body systems that are vibrating at the optimal frequency are healthy and full of vitality. But, when we hold on to trapped emotions, have consistent negative thoughts, stay in unhealthy relationships or eat unhealthily, those energies get stored in the body and lower our vibrational frequency. There are optimal frequencies for all parts of the body, and over time having them vibrate lower than normal, leads to illness. Remember that at its source the energy is one of pure light, love and information. Once we transmute that energy into denser energy states through our thoughts, negative emotions and identification, we lower our vibrational frequency. Keeping a calm mind, open heart, and stable body we are able to maintain that energy closer to that of its source.

The Energy Systems

There are many different energy systems in the body that form our energy matrix. Many of the modalities, such as Healing Touch and Reiki, deal with the chakra system, whereas something like Acupuncture deals with meridians. Chakras are spinning wheels of energy. There are seven major chakras and many minor ones throughout the body. An energy practitioner can assess the health of the chakras and clear and balance them when necessary.

The major chakras of the body begin at the base of the spine and move upward. The lower three chakras include: the first chakra found at the base of the spine, the second at the lower abdomen and the third chakra, which is located below the sternum. These three chakras correspond to the physical, material realm. The upper three chakras the fifth, sixth, and seventh, are located at the throat, the third eye and the crown of the head, respectively. These chakras correspond to the higher spiritual realms. The fourth chakra or the heart center is the bridge between the two. In order for any healing to occur, we need to have an open heart. This means we need to move from a space of unconditional love for ourselves, others and the planet. This is paramount to our survival and again will not be recognized until we can still our minds. There is so much information waiting for us from our guides, our highest self and even from God, if we are calm and still enough to listen. All information about our own health and subsequent healing can be known when we move from this space. It is also the single most important factor in the survival of the human race. All of us are connected through this field. Every action taken against one another serves to create distortions. It affects us all on an energetic level. The key is to open the bridge that is to say the heart, and all the rest will become self-evident.

From a pragmatic level, how do we use this understanding to create healing in the body? It always begins with the ability to be present and conscious. Energy flows where intention goes. Speaking in terms of targeted healing, use your intention and hold yourself in love. Imagine life force coming in through the crown of your head (crown chakra) and flowing out through the palms of your hands. Set your intention for love and healing to come to you in your highest good. The thing to remember is that where the physical manifestation exists, for example your angina, may not be where the root cause is. Remembering back to chapter one, we are holistic beings, and the physical ailment may not be the root of your issue. From an Energy Medicine perspective, if all things originally start out in the field and move inwards, the cause might be far different from the physical manifestation. In my sessions, I always ask that the energy go where the need for healing is greatest and always ask for healing in my client's highest good.

In my Meditation for Self Healing class, I teach people about how to do healing work with chakras as a means of self-care. I know that the research is not available to fully support my claims, but I urge you to do the Ball of Energy Exercise in the appendix and then ask you to keep an open mind. Not all information comes through logic and research. We know in our hearts that there is more than just what our five senses can detect or our instruments can measure. I mentioned in the last section that everything has a vibrational frequency. We can use light, sound, and color for our own healing and those same things can affect the functioning of the chakras.[3] In my work, I have given mandalas to clients to use as the focus of their meditations that correspond to the chakras that need alignment. You can do yoga asanas that open up the chakra system. You can eat foods to balance chakras. There are so many possibilities for self-healing once you make the connections between our spiritual and energetic nature and the health of the body.

Understanding the field of consciousness is the first and most important step. Of course, it is also important to recognize when you need outside help. An energy practitioner can help you to bring balance to the energy field. Seek one out, especially if what I am saying in this chapter is new information to you.

Heart-Based Living

The Institute of Heart Math has been doing amazing work in understanding how the brain and the heart communicate with each other.[4] Through their research they discovered that the heart has the ability to bring the brain and other organs into a state called coherence. They are working on a project called The Global Coherence Initiative that aims to bring the world into coherence through sustained positive emotion. It is their goal to shift the global consciousness towards cooperation, stability and empathy through their heart-centered approach, bringing about global peace and individual healing.

The closer we move to understanding our spiritual nature, stripping away the workings of the ego, the more we move toward the health and healing of the body and the planet. The name of my lifelong vision for my work is Hestia Health. Hestia was a Greek goddess who believed in a life of quiet contemplation and her focus was on the simple things in life. Her name means, essence. The symbol of Hestia is the eternal flame. Most people think she represents only domestic duties, but she was about getting the center of her life in order, moving from her center, to her family, to her town and outward. It starts with us as individuals.

We are sensory beings, some more visual, more auditory or more tactile, but multi-sensory nonetheless. We need to move away from our thinking that there is a hierarchal structure where the mind always presides over the body. The body is able to communicate to the mind by way of the spirit. It is the spirit that allows the sensation of the body to be experienced by the mind. The mind communicates to the body, but its language is flow, the flow of the spirit. This is why illness is a message and in many cases a gift. It brings to your attention the break down in this communication and healing may not occur until you can reestablish this connection.

The resistance to the flow of the spirit is manifesting itself in more and more ways. Whether we acknowledge it or not, we are evolving. Our consciousness is evolving - this is the nature of things. What once satisfied us, is no longer serving our collective will to move forward. This is one of the reasons why we see such a breakdown in our health that we didn't see fifty or one hundred years ago. We require more - our consciousness demands it. We think that we can evolve through technology alone. The people of Western society are trying as hard as they might to dampen it; the Tao, the flow, the force, the way, and that is why we see diseases of lifestyle, or diseases of choice. We need stillness of the mind to create health in the body and healing to our planet. In this stillness we experience our connection – our oneness with each other and the earth. Not to belabor the point too much, but survival is a poignant issue right now, even if we choose not to see it. We must evolve, we must wake up and see the truths that are right there, nagging us just below the surface, creating the resistance in the body.

Chapter 16

Where Spirit Meets Science:
Our New Focus

Where do we go from here? How do we truly connect our bodies and mind to the spirit? And most importantly, how does that connection change our health, and the world? To not fully understand the connection, will be our greatest human error. It will truly lead to our downfall as a civilization. Once we understand consciousness and our connectedness, change can happen in an instant. Disease is resistance. Over and over we choose to ignore our feelings, intuitions, our desires. We eat food that our bodies resist, we allow roles and circumstance to define us and we move through life on autopilot. It is this imbalance that allows us to live in unhealthy bodies, and limiting mindsets. We can no longer afford to dismiss and deny the cumulative effects of our actions. The earth is facing large-scale environmental problems, water shortages, pollution and unsustainable use of our resources. Because we fail to understand, for example, how issues in the oceans affect us, we fail to see how resource depletion and exploitation corrupts us. Our bodies are paying the price. So how does this information or perspective change our health care? Let's review the things that lead to the creation of the optimal healing environment.

- Creative movement by using our bodies every single day in creative ways that provide us with the essentials of life.

- A whole food, regional diet that regards food as our medicine.

- Stress reduction that incorporates informal and formal practices of mindfulness and opportunities to develop a calm mind.

- The cultivation and awareness of ourselves as spiritual/energetic beings. In that, we understand the importance of balance, purpose, connection and appropriate allocations of our personal resources.

- Engage in right thinking, becoming mindful of our thoughts and emotions and the effect that they have on the body. We learn to surrender and release when it is appropriate, to maintain a calm mind and an open heart. These are the keys to our health.

    Our current system looks at disease, not wellness or prevention. It looks at symptoms, not the root cause. It knows about nutrition, but chooses cheap over whole; convenient over real. It is alarming to me that we serve processed foods in hospitals, we know better and still choose unwisely. It is the mass production of everything that took the essence out of food, and the nutrition. It also caused the biggest threat to the environment. The system needs to reboot, go back to community living - a smaller business-based local economy. It is how we reestablish social connection, gives us back our sense of purpose, and allows us to use our bodies more for the fundamentals of existence. Ultimately, will people have to give up their Starbuck's latte? Maybe. Only to be replaced by a local shop with local products. Or maybe Starbuck's will find a way to do that themselves.

Now let me make myself perfectly clear. This will never work as a government mandated endeavor. One of my favorite sayings is, "You can't spread democracy through invasion". This change needs to be accompanied by a collective shift in consciousness, not through legislation. Once we understand our connectedness, this is possible. In an instant, this is possible and more increasingly than ever, necessary. This isn't about a new world order or a one-world government, but about each individual choosing, opting for something different - something more meaningful than the status quo. We cannot turn a blind eye any longer. We need to start becoming aware of how our food is made, how our choices and thirst for stuff affects people on the other side of the world. Evaluating and becoming aware of why we make the choices we make and seeing how we could choose different, more wisely. I truly believe that if we searched our hearts, we would.

All throughout history and in every part of the world, religions have been created. Why? On some level we have always known that there is something more. Now we have perverted this understanding to an alarming degree in what we have done in the name of religion. But, we have always felt there was something more, a binding agent that connects us, but we resisted, twisted and exploited this knowing and desire. Let's choose different. Instead of resisting this, let's open ourselves up to it.

The New Frontiers

The two new frontiers of medicine to be explored and propagated are Mind/Body Medicine and Energy Medicine. They are interconnected and interdependent. There will be huge resistance to this change. There is not a lot of money to be made from the flourishing of either one of these, only the flourishing of the human spirit. Right now we have the balance of our health and the planet in the hands of a (relative) few, but it needs to be in our hands, the people's hands. The thing is we are the creators of everything right, but we are also the creators of everything wrong. We need to take responsibility for our lack of accountability as individuals, as a country and as a world. We have the technology now to pass information over the globe in seconds, this has never been possible before now. There are no excuses anymore not to understand the plight of the earth and all humans living on this planet. Our heads and our bodies are aching with the truth. If we think of the world as a body, and whichever country you reside in as the heart. Imagine that all the other nations are spread out through the body. It makes it harder to cut off a limb once you know it is connected to you. We already feel the pain, but we have been shutting out – we have been resisting the knowledge.

Let's open our hearts and minds to the inner voices. Let us hear what they have to say in the solitude. I'm not sure what it will look like once we wake up, but I know this, what we are doing does not feel right, sound or equitable. We cannot just Band-Aid the symptoms any longer. Inner peace is something we have all been searching for on a global level - depression, anxiety, heart disease, inflammation and cancer are manifestations of this resistance.

HEALING ENVIRONMENT

Doctors need to be educated in Energy Medicine, Mind/Body Medicine, environmental toxicity, food production and nutrition. At their core they got into medicine to help people heal and we should really give them the opportunity to do so. To really create change, they to need nurture their bond with their patients by taking time to breathe with them. They need to be mindful listeners. As mentioned, if we can calm the person at a cellular level, we create the environment for greatness. We won't be able to listen without limiting the mental, physical and emotional congestion that is occurring in our bodies. It is not about better technology, surgeries and drugs, it is about quieting the mind. We store memories in every cell, muscle, organ and energetic field, we have the wisdom of the ages literally running through our bodies, but we will not heed the call until we can hear the phone ringing. If we do not answer the call, I am afraid within decades, the earth will begin to make decisions for us. She is already warning us of things to come. Though man is great, the Mother Earth is greater. She will not sacrifice all of life for us, nor should she have to. She embodies the universal truths. They are imbedded in her on a cellular, spiritual and energetic level as well. Her patience is long, but her action will be swift.

I do not want to be considered a fear monger; in fact I am an eternal idealist. I really think we can evoke a change. There is a reason there has been an influx of news, television programs, etc. on these topics, it is because people already know that the time for change is upon us. Many of us have been waiting for it since the day of our births. I am left with the dilemma, if I do not warn of some of the tragic outcomes of our actions, then people might continue to live in the dark, and if I do I am prompting change out of fear. This is never my intention. All I ask is that people spend a few moments in solitude and make decisions from the place of inner awareness. But I don't know if most of us can find a quiet place in their mind, without first having a desire for inner peace. Inner peace requires mindfulness as a component, a presence that most people have not yet mastered. So, alas it is the state of the human condition that until there is clear and present danger people will never be motivated to change. Especially, the type of change that I am proposing; a new paradigm, a total upheaval of everything we now hold dear. Are you ready to get off the polarity rollercoaster - to make conscious choices? Take what I say and hold it in your heart space. If it resonates with you, then look in to it further, see what it means for you. If it doesn't resonate, then ask yourself why and look into that.

It has always been hard for me to separate the parts from the whole. So, I could not write a book about our health without the discussion of the whole. The whole being, the mind/body spirit connection and the environmental, spiritual and even political impact of our choices. It is all connected. Open your hearts and quiet your mind and the answers will come to you. Maybe those answers will not be the same as mine and maybe that is the point, but let's start the discussion on a global scale. We have the opportunity to create and engage in this global discussion not via our representatives, but through the Internet. I am not an engineer or a biologist or an architect, but you are, so bring your ideas to the table. Don't let politics convince you to choose a side, see all sides and decide for yourself. This isn't about power, or money or greed. It is not some end game used to perpetuate my interests. It is about the common interest that heals our bodies, our earth and our hearts. There is enough, there is abundance, there is a way, but we need to act now- consciously & deliberately. Lose the attachments to material goods and status; they do not fulfill us on any level.

What I am saying may sound insurmountable to you, but we can begin this shift through our health. Use YOUR health as a catalyst, use the tools given to you in this book. If we could get hospitals, public health educators and schools to teach about food as medicine, mindfulness, meditation, and the importance of the mind/body connection, we can make a difference. We know the benefits that these have in prevention and in self-care. If we put the emphasis on how our thoughts affect the physiology of the body. If we bring attention to the ills of stress and give people tools for relaxation. You wouldn't even need to discuss God or Spirit because I know that at this stage it would never be accepted in public education. But if we can teach people how to open their hearts and calm their minds, these truths will become evident. Our health is a manifestation of the current state of affairs, so lets use our health to get us out of it. There are ways to introduce these concepts to the public from a purely health related standpoint. We don't have to think about changing the whole world, we just need to heal ourselves.

Let's invite the abstract, the emotional, and the intuitive back into our daily lives. In fact, let's celebrate them. Let us appreciate the whole, and not always strive for the dichotomies. As I mentioned, it was these opposites that catapulted our ingenuity and innovations, but we have to bring it back together. There is the knowledge in the whole - the wisdom of the entire universe is there and ready for us to have. The earth requires us to WAKE UP!

On every level and in every system we need to become whole. Find the inner peace by creating balance first in our minds, bodies and spirits. Then we must create harmony in our food, water and energy systems. They are in crisis because we are in crisis and vice versa. Connection and collaboration must drive our efforts. We have the opportunity, the ability and the duty to get it together. As humans we are given so many gifts and abilities paralleled only by our unconscious fear. The time is now. The choice is ours and the consequence of inaction is steep. We must move forward - consciously. Now it is your turn.

Appendix

The Optimal Healing Environment

Stress Reduction: Engage in stress reduction techniques everyday. The aim is to bring balance to the body/mind and spirit. (See chapter 4 for details)

Physical Activity – Be physically active almost everyday. Try to accumulate 150mins of activity per week. Include strength exercises and stretching 2-3 days per week. (See chapter 6 for details)

Consider Your Food as Medicine – Eat a diet rich in whole organic foods (preferably) according to your specific needs. (See chapter 7 for details)

Right Thinking - Start to be a conscious healer. Become more aware of your thoughts in relations to how they affect your body. (See section 3 on the mind)

Spiritual and Energetic Growth – All healing relates to your chosen path here on earth. Tune in to your spiritual side and allow it to develop and mature. (See section 4 on the spirit)

HEALING ENVIRONMENT

Progressive Relaxation

Now begin to become aware of your breathing.....Not trying to control it, but allow it to move freely and easily through your body. Moving in and out as you begin to move inward. Focusing on the breath. Notice the rise and fall of your ribcage, the quality and depth of your breath. You are beginning to feel calm and relaxed.

 Now begin taking deeper breaths in through your nose and out through your nose. Drawing the breath deep down into the belly, allowing the belly to expand with the inhalation and gently fall toward the spine on the exhalation. Becoming aware of how this deep breath is nourishing the body and the mind.

Now I want you to imagine the room is filling with a beautiful white light. This light is one of love, peace and healing. Now imagine as you draw in the breath deep into the belly, that you also draw in this healing light. As this light begins to move inward, it pushes out any unwanted stress or negativity. Feel the warmth, love and health of this beautiful white light and with each breath you draw in light, you breathe out stress....

Now turn your attention to the top of your head. Feel the warmth of the light as it illuminates the top of your scalp, and spreads slowly downwards....Feel the muscles around the eyes release. Notice how it feels for your eyebrows to begin resting, as your forehead becomes relaxed and smooth. Feel your eyelids becoming very heavy..... more relaxed.... as you breathe in light, you breathe out stress. Enjoy the feeling of deep relaxation and calm. Becoming very calm and very relaxed.

Now imagine the light moving down to your jaw... let your jaw relax by allowing your teeth to be slightly apart while your lips are gently touching.... Allow your tongue to roll gently and naturally back in your mouth.

Now this beautiful white light continues to flow downward, now illuminating your neck.... allow a feeling of relaxation to begin at the top of your neck, and flow downward...as the muscles begin to release and relax in the warmth and calm of the light.

Feel the relaxation as your shoulders release tension and become loose.... Let your shoulders gently sink downward.... Feel your collar bones becoming relaxed as your shoulders move gently back, and your chest widens slightly...Allow all the muscles in your shoulders to feel smooth... and relaxed.... the muscles release as you breathe in light, you breath out stress.

Notice your breathing once again... see how regular it has become... continue to take slow.... smooth.... deep breaths... Breathe in the feeling of relaxation, light, health and healing.... and breathe out any tension... Now continue to imagine this beautiful white light as it illuminates your right arm..... Feel the relaxation flowing as the warmth and the light move down from your right shoulder.... allow your upper arm to relax... your elbow.... lower arm... and wrist as they release and relax.... As you breathe in light you breathe out stress.

Enjoy the feeling of relaxation as the muscles of your right arm release and relax.... Feel the warmth of the light flowing into your hand... Let all the tension drain out each finger tip and melt away.... the relaxation spreads to your thumb... index finger.... middle finger... ring finger... and little finger....

Feel the warmth and light flowing down your left arm... Let the muscles of the left upper arm release and relax.... Relax your elbow.... lower arm.... and wrist.... Feel the relaxation flowing down your left arm....Let all the tension melt away.... imagine the tension flowing right out your fingertips... Allow your left hand to relax completely.... relax your thumb... index finger.... middle finger... ring finger... and little finger....

HEALING ENVIRONMENT

Both of your arms are now totally relaxed... filling you with a sense of peace and calm, health and healing as you breathe in light, you breathe out stress...

Now imagine this beautiful white light illuminating your chest and abdomen...feel the warmth of this beautiful white light as you bring your attention and breath to that space.... feel the relaxation there... becoming deeper with each and every breath...Now turn your attention to your upper back... Feel the light flow down your spine... Let all the muscles in that area release and relax.... relax your upper back... middle back and lower back.... allow your back to release and relax as all the tension and all the stress melts away..... Feel the deep sense of peace and relaxation in your whole upper body ....as you breathe in light and breathe out stress.

Now imagine the beautiful white light has illuminated your hip muscles. Feel the warmth as the muscles release and relax... Relax all the way from your buttocks, down the back of your thighs...allowing all the tension and all the stress to melt away. Bring the warmth of the light and your breath to relax the muscles on the front of your thighs... Feel the relaxation in your upper legs flowing down to your knees... your calves and shins.... your ankles.... and your feet.... allow all the muscles to release and relax as all the tension and all the stress just melt away in your lower body. As you breathe in light, you breathe out stress.

Allow any last bits of tension to flow right out the soles of your feet.... Feel the beautiful white light flowing through your entire body... From the top of your head... down to the bottoms of your feet...you are illuminated with this beautiful light of love, health and healing. Take a moment to scan your body to see if there is any remaining tension to let go. Bring the light and the breath into that space and allow the light to dissolve any tension or stress. Enjoy the feeling of total relaxation.....peace and calm.

Memorize this feeling so you can re-create this relaxed state whenever you wish....and when you are ready, start to bring your attention back to the room. Begin to become more aware and alert, allowing this calm feeling to remain in the body and the mind to stay clear. Begin to wiggle your fingers and toes and when you are ready, slowly get up and move around.

Meditation Exercise #1

Belly Breathing on the Beach

Lie down to begin this meditation. Place hands on the lower abdomen, just below the navel.

Focus in on the breath, taking a few regular breaths in the beginning.

Bring your focus inwards, following the breath without controlling it.

Begin to breathe deeper through the nose and imagine drawing the breath deep down into the belly.

As you inhale and draw the breath into the belly, allow the breath to fill the belly causing it to gently push the belly outward.

As you exhale completely, allow the belly to fall back toward the spine, your hands will fall toward the spine as well. Your hands should rise and fall with the breath.

Find your own rhythm and as you get better at this there should be a wave like movement of the torso. As you begin to find that wave like rhythm, imagine yourself laying on the beach.

Take time to visualize the sight, sounds and smells of the beach. Feel the warmth of the sun, listen to the birds off in the distance, feel the calming warm breeze.

Bring your attention to the ocean waves, and as the waves come in, breathe in and as the waves go out, breathe out. Allow the waves to wash over you releasing all the tension out of your body with each exhalation.

Continue to a sense of completion.

Meditation Exercise #2

Beginner's Meditation

Sit in a comfortable position and begin by focusing on your breath.

Take a few regular breaths, but start to bring attention to the breath.

Begin to breathe deeper (through the nose), focusing in on the inhalation and the exhalation. Take a few extra moments longer on the exhalation to exhale completely.

If your mind wanders bring attention back to the breath.

Become aware of how the breath changes the body i.e. how the rib cage moves, how the breath sounds on the exhalation, where the breath is drawn in to or out of and/or how the abdomen moves.

Continue to a sense of completion.

Mediation Exercise #3

Finding Your Place of Power

Use a previous meditation exercise to bring yourself into a calm and mindful state.

Take a moment to create your perfect peaceful setting. There is no right place, it could be a beach or a meadow, it is up to you, but always use the images that arise. Don't force them or over think them. They could provide clues to your subconscious.

Explore it, notice how it smells, looks, tastes and feels. Again do this without judgment or reflection. Finally, once you have gotten a feel for your surroundings, find a place to rest.

This place should make you feel calm, centered and at peace.

Feel the energy of the earth come up through your tailbone and feel the energy come down from the heavens into the top of your head (i.e. the crown chakra).

Feel how this connection to the earth and the sky balances you and brings you back to center. This is a place where deep relaxation and healing can occur. Spend some time in this spot to allow your body to become revitalized.

When you are finished, slowly bring your awareness back to the room you are in.

Once you are good at imagining this place, this is a tool you can use over and over again to bring yourself into a deeply relaxed and balanced state.

Meditation Exercise #4

Color Breathing for Pain Control

Sit in a comfortable position and begin using the belly breathing.

Focus your attention on your where your pain is located. If you were to pick a color to describe that pain, what would it be? E.g. Red

Now pick a calming and cooling color that represents healing and comfort to you. E.g. Light blue.

HEALING ENVIRONMENT

On the inhalation, draw in the cooling color and bring it to the pain center. Feel the cooling sensation that floods that area. Notice how it brings you relief.

On the exhalation, breath out the pain color with the intention that the color/pain is beginning to be released and removed from that space and is being replaced by the calming and cooling color.

As you continue, imagine the pain color moving farther and farther away from the body.

Continue until the pain is gone or has become more manageable.

The red/blue colors are just suggestions, use colors that feel right to you. The more you practice this technique, the better it will work.

Meditation Exercise #5

The Staircase of Relaxation

This meditation can be done lying down and is ideal to do before bedtime to quiet the mind before sleep.

Take three deep cleansing breaths, breathing in through the nose and out through the mouth.

Close your eyes and begin to move your focus inward.

Imagine yourself at the top of a staircase that has ten steps. Take a moment to see your staircase. Take note of what it looks like, what it is made of and any other characteristics that are imagined.

Then imagine as you descend the staircase (holding on to a sturdy banister) that each step takes you into a deeper state of relaxation. Once you reach the bottom of the staircase, you will be in a calm and relaxed state.

Notice that as you take each step you become more calm, at peace, and centered. If you wish, you can combine this meditation with Mediation Exercise #3 - Finding Your Place of Power

Meditation Exercise #6

Ball of Energy Meditation

I urge everyone to do this meditation as the first step towards knowing yourself as an energetic being.

While standing or sitting, take a few moments with your attention at your feet. Move the toes around and get the feeling of being grounded.

Then take three deep breaths, drawing the breaths in through the nose and out through the mouth.

Continue breathing in through the nose and exhaling through the nose. Now imagine drawing energy up through the feet on the inhalation and the energy moving through the palms of the hands on the exhalation.

Try doing this with the eyes open and then closed. Beginning to notice what sensations are going on in the body.

Now rub the hands vigorously together and hold the palms of the hands about one inch apart. Slowly move the palms of the hands farther apart and then slowly back together. Especially become aware of how the breath changes the sensations in the hands.

As you do this exercise you will notice that the sensation between the hands is growing stronger. It may be felt as heat, tingling, or the feeling of two magnets repelling one another.

Try to create a ball of energy. Once you have formed a ball you can imagine holding yourself in the ball for your own healing, imagine holding someone else in the ball that may need healing or imagine the whole world receiving this healing ball of energy.

Once you feel done, gently thank God or the Universe for the beautiful experience and shift the energy back to the earth for her healing.

Meditation Exercise #7

Vase Breathing

This is a good meditation for rejuvenation of all the seven major chakras.

Follow the preceding instruction on basic breathing. Once you are in a calm and relaxed state use the following imagery to bring about relaxation and healing.

Imagine a hollow tube that runs from the top of your head and balloons out in your lower abdomen i.e. like a vase. As with any imagery you use, really take the time in the beginning to visualize the light, feel the heat and become aware of all of its characteristics without reflecting on them.

Imagine with each breath you draw in light, deep into your belly. Imagine as you exhale that you are removing stress. Visualize that as the light comes in, the unwanted elements are pushed out.

As you continue to breathe in light, the base of the vase begins to fill and then the tube also begins to fill, until it is filled in its entirety with light.

Upon filling with light, the tube becomes overwhelmed and the light then begins to branch out into the rest of your body. Filing all the organs, vessels and cells with this light, remembering that on every exhalation you continue to remove any unwanted stress or tension.

At this point you are completely illuminated with light. Take your awareness to any specific place in your body that needs special care and use the image of light and your breath to dissolve any unresolved issues within the body.

Meditation Exercise #8

The Semi Permeable Cell

It is important to clear and balance your own energy system, but many times we don't realize that much of the negativity, anxiety or depressive thoughts may be the result of the people around us. Again, this requires a level of awareness; to know what is your junk and what is other people's junk. Once you know the culprits, either situational or specifically, do this exercise. Before entering a situation that may drain or suck energy from you, spend a few moments breathing deeply and getting centered.

Wiggle your toes, bringing attention to your feet and feel the ground beneath you.

Bring your attention to your heart space and imagine a glowing egg that originates in the heart and then extends out around your body. This is a declaration of your boundaries.

Spend a few moments and bless the person or situation that may cause you negativity or discomfort, and wish them their highest good.

Spend a few breaths there until you are comfortable with the visualization.

Then set your intention for the situation. E.g. It is my intention to maintain my energetic integrity and I only allow the other person (and/or your situation) access to my energy with my permission and with my highest good in mind.

Meditation Exercise #9

Increasing Your Intuition

It is important to develop your inner knowing. This like any skill takes practice. Your intuition is a function of the sixth chakra, your third eye. Practice this meditation to open up to your inner knowing and guidance. Remember that intuition in itself is not the end game; it is what you use your intuition for that makes it spiritual.

Candle Light Meditation

Place a lit candle about three feet in front of you and with your eyes closed, begin to do some basic breathing to create a calm mindful state, bringing your focus to your heart center.

Once you feel calm and centered, open your eyes and focus on the candle, now bringing your focus up to your third eye chakra. Look at the candle with a relaxed focus and blink only when necessary.

Close your eyes, when and if it feels right to do so, maintain the image of the candle in your third eye. Allow whatever images, colors, sights and sounds to arise without judgment.

Try to maintain the image of the flame for as long as possible, but without struggle.

Continue to a sense of completion.

Meditation Exercise #10

Chakra Meditation

I want to give you images to hold in your mind that will awaken the chakras. Set the intention that you want to use these images to create balance and proper flow in your chakras for your highest good. Go ahead and change the images if it feels right. Once you are in a calm and relaxed state use the following imagery to bring about the opening and activation of each chakra.

Focus on the area of each of the chakras as you allow your attention and breath to move to that area. Allow the following images to open and activate each chakra. Really take a moment to visualize all the characteristics of the image, and allow those characteristics to resonate in the specific chakra area.

- Root Chakra - A Red Rose

- Sacral Chakra - An Orange Marigold

- Solar Plexus - A Yellow Daffodil

- Heart Chakra - Green Grass

- Throat Chakra - Bluebells

- Third Eye Chakra - A Violet

- Crown Chakra - A White Lotus

For more resources visit www.hestiahealth.com

Notes

Chapter 1

[1] Zollman, C., and A. Vickers. "ABC of Complementary Medicine: What Is Complementary Medicine?" *BMJ* 319, no. 7211 (September 11, 1999): 693–696.

[2] Weil, Andrew. *Spontaneous Healing: How to Discover and Enhance Your Body's Natural Ability to Maintain and Heal Itself.* 1st ed. New York: Knopf, 1995. 109

[3] Carrico, Mara. "Yoga Journal - Yoga Basics Column - The Eight Limbs." Online Magazine. *Yoga Journal*, n.d. http://www.yogajournal.com/basics/158.

[4] Isaac, Katherine M.D. "One Day in Mind/Body Medicine", Massachusetts General Hospital, Boston, MA, November 8, 2010.

[5] Chopra, Deepak. *Ageless Body, Timeless Mind : the Quantum Alternative to Growing Old.* 1st ed. New York: Harmony Books, 1993. 19.

[6] Weil, Andrew M.D. *Health and Healing.* New York, New York: Houghton Mifflin Company, 1995. 65-71.

[7] Purves, William, Craig Heller, Gordon Orians, and David Sadava. *Life : the Science of Biology.* 6th ed. Sunderland Massachusetts: Sinauer Associates, 2001. 699.

[8] Baldwin, Christina. *Life's Companion: Journal Writing as a Spiritual Quest.* Bantam, 1990. 67.

Chapter 2

[1] Benson, Herbert M.D. "One Day in Mind/Body Medicine", Massachusetts General Hospital, Boston, MA, November 8, 2010.

[2] Gilbert, Elizabeth. *Eat, Pray, Love : One Woman's Search for Everything Across Italy, India and Indonesia.* New York: Viking, 2006. 61.

[3] "Middle Class Families Eat MORE Fast Food Than Poor Ones, Study Claims." *Mail Online*, n.d. http://www.dailymail.co.uk/sciencetech/article-2058631/Study-shows-slimmer-middle-class-eats-fast-food-obese-poor.html.

Chapter 3

[1] Moving&shaking. "HAPPENINGS AT MUSE: Town Hall Meeting." *HAPPENINGS AT MUSE*, February 11, 2010. http://musestudios.blogspot.com/2010/02/town-hall-meeting.html.

[2] *Dan Buettner: How to Live to Be 100+ | Video on TED.com*, n.d. http://www.ted.com/talks/dan_buettner_how_to_live_to_be_100.html.

[3] Ornish, Dean. *Love and Survival: 8 Pathways to Intimacy and Health.* 1st ed. William Morrow Paperbacks, 1999. 1.

[4] Egolf, B, J Lasker, S Wolf, and L Potvin. "The Roseto Effect: a 50-year Comparison of Mortality Rates." *American Journal of Public Health* 82, no. 8 (August 1992): 1089–1092.

[5] Achterberg, Jeanne, Karin Cooke, Todd Richards, Leanna J. Standish, Leila Kozak, and James Lake. "Evidence for Correlations Between Distant Intentionality and Brain Function in Recipients: A Functional Magnetic

Resonance Imaging Analysis." *The Journal of Alternative and Complementary Medicine* 11, no. 6 (December 2005): 965–971.
6 Cohen, Sheldon, and Thomas A. Wills. "Stress, Social Support, and the Buffering Hypothesis." *Psychological Bulletin* 98, no. 2 (1985): 310–357.
7 "Media Multitaskers Pay Mental Price, Stanford Study Shows", August 24, 2009. http://news.stanford.edu/news/2009/august24/multitask-research-study-082409.html.
8 Chopra, Deepak. *Ageless Body, Timeless Mind : the Quantum Alternative to Growing Old*. 1st ed. New York: Harmony Books, 1993.
9 Travaline, John M., Robert Ruchinskas, and Gilbert E. D'Alonzo. "Patient-Physician Communication: Why and How." *JAOA: Journal of the American Osteopathic Association* 105, no. 1 (January 1, 2005): 13–18.
10 "Attunement." *The Free Dictionary*, n.d.

11 Brickman, P, D Coates, and R Janoff-Bulman. "Lottery Winners and Accident Victims: Is Happiness Relative?" *Journal of Personality and Social Psychology* 36, no. 8 (August 1978): 917–927.
12 "Feeling Like Your Life Has Purpose May Protect Against Alzheimer's." *Fisher Center for Alzheimer's Research Foundation*, n.d. http://www.alzinfo.org/05/articles/prevention-and-wellness-2.
13 "UnitedHealth Group - News - Volunteers Report Improved Physical, Emotional Health", n.d. http://www.unitedhealthgroup.com/newsroom/news.aspx?id=e5cb9326-8c3e-43cd-bd5d-802620037227.

Chapter 4
1 Hansen, Bente. *The New World of Self-Healing: Awakening the Chakras & Rejuvenating Your Energy Field*. Llewellyn Publications, 2006.
2 "The 7,000km Journey That Links Amazon Destruction to Fast Food." *The Guardian*, April 6, 2006. http://www.guardian.co.uk/business/2006/apr/06/brazil.food.
3 News, Bloomberg. "McDonald's to Open a Restaurant a Day in China in Four Years." *Bloomberg*, n.d. http://www.bloomberg.com/news/2011-07-29/mcdonald-s-franchises-to-account-for-up-to-20-of-china-business.html.
4 Koons, Deborah. *The Future of Food*. Documentary, N/A.
5 Brown, Lester R. *Plan B 2.0: Rescuing a Planet Under Stress and a Civilization in Trouble*. Revised. W. W. Norton, 2006. 89.
6 "You Are What You Grow", n.d. http://michaelpollan.com/articles-archive/you-are-what-you-grow/.

7 McDonald, David. "Docs for Docs: Online with the NFB." *CMAJ : Canadian Medical Association Journal* 181, no. 6–7 (September 2009): 400–401.

[8] "WHO | WHO Issues Revised Drinking-water Guidelines to Prevent Waterborne Disease." *WHO*, n.d. http://www.who.int/water_sanitation_health/events/press_backgrounder/en/.

[9] "2011 Gulf of Mexico 'Dead Zone' Could Be Biggest Ever." *ScienceDaily*, n.d. http://www.sciencedaily.com/releases/2011/07/110718141618.htm.

[10] "Clean Water Crisis, Water Crisis Facts, Water Crisis Resources - National Geographic." *National Geographic*, n.d. http://environment.nationalgeographic.com/environment/freshwater/freshwater-crisis/.

[11] Mascarelli, Amanda. "Demand for Water Outstrips Supply." *Nature* (August 8, 2012). http://www.nature.com/news/demand-for-water-outstrips-supply-1.11143.

[12] "Fracking in Colorado Uses a City's Worth of Water, Enviro Report Says - Denver Business Journal", n.d. http://www.bizjournals.com/denver/news/2012/06/20/fracking-in-colorado-uses-a-citys.html?page=all.

[13] "Fracking in Colorado Uses a City's Worth of Water, Enviro Report Says - Denver Business Journal", n.d. http://www.bizjournals.com/denver/news/2012/06/20/fracking-in-colorado-uses-a-citys.html?page=all.

[14] "Powerful US Congressman Sends Serious Opposition to Canada Oil Sands Pipeline", n.d. http://www.desmogblog.com/powerful-democratic-congressman-sends-serious-opposition-canada-oil-sands-pipeline.

[15] Wikipedia contributors. "Corporatocracy." *Wikipedia, the Free Encyclopedia*. Wikimedia Foundation, Inc., September 13, 2012. http://en.wikipedia.org/w/index.php?title=Corporatocracy&oldid=509750430.

[16] Achbar, Mark, and Jennifer Abbott. *The Corporation*. Documentary, History, 2004.

[17] "Global Heritage Fund | GHF", n.d. http://globalheritagefund.org/our_approach/poverty_facts.

Chapter 5

[1] Selye, Hans. *Stress Without Distress*. [1st ed.]. Philadelphia: Lippincott, 1974.

[2] Benjamin, Ben, Ph.D., and Ruth Werner. "You and Your Nervous System: How Stress Affects Your Body." *Health Touch News*, 2009.

[3] Kiecolt-Glaser, J.K., P.T. Marucha, A.M. Mercado, W.B. Malarkey, and R. Glaser. "Slowing of Wound Healing by Psychological Stress." *The Lancet* 346, no. 8984 (November 4, 1995): 1194–1196.

[4] "Task-oriented Versus Emotion-oriented Coping Strategies: The Case of College Students", 2005. http://findarticles.com/p/articles/mi_m0FCR/is_1_39/ai_n13603935/pg

    _4/?tag=content;col1.
[5] Fass, Nancy. "Are You Getting Enough Sleep." *Boosting Immunity : Creating Wellness Naturally*. Len Saputo and Nancy Fass. Novato Calif.: New World Library, 2002. 29.
[6] Cohen, Sheldon, and Thomas A. Wills. "Stress, Social Support, and the Buffering Hypothesis." *Psychological Bulletin* 98, no. 2 (1985): 310–357.
[7] Hypnosis Motivation Institute. *Foundations in Hypnotherapy*. Online Distance Education. Foundations in Hypnotherapy, n.d.
[8] Baldwin, Christina. *Life's Companion: Journal Writing as a Spiritual Quest*. Bantam, 1990. 214.
[9] Goldstein, Joseph. *Insight Meditation : the Practice of Freedom*. 1st ed. Boston ;;London ;[New York N.Y.]: Shambhala ;;Distributed in the U.S. by Random House, 1993. 71.

Chapter 6

[1] "Treasure Valley Y." Community Organization. *YMCA Treasure Valley Idaho*, n.d. http://www.ymcatvidaho.org/.
[2] Payne, Larry. *Yoga Rx : a Step-by-step Program to Promote Health, Wellness, and Healing for Common Ailments*. 1st ed. New York: Broadway Books, 2002. 34.
[3] Chopra, Deepak. *Ageless Body, Timeless Mind : the Quantum Alternative to Growing Old*. 1st ed. New York: Harmony Books, 1993. 13.
[4] Purves, William, Sadava, David, Orians, Gordon, and Heller, Craig. *Life : the Science of Biology*. 6th ed. Sunderland Massachusetts: Sinauer Associates, 2001. 699.
[5] Canadian Society of Exercise Physiologists. "CSEP - Get the Guidelines." Professional Organization. *CSEP*, n.d. http://csep.ca/english/view.asp?x=804.
[6] Weil, Andrew. *Spontaneous Healing : How to Discover and Enhance Your Body's Natural Ability to Maintain and Heal Itself*. 1st ed. New York: Knopf, 1995. 187.
[7] Castaneda, Carlos. *Journey to Ixtlan: The Lessons of Don Juan*. Washington Square Press, 1991.
[8] Brosse A.L., Sheets E.S., Lett H.S., and Blumenthal J.A. "Exercise and the Treatment of Clinical Depression in Adults: Recent Findings and Future Directions." *Sports Medicine* 32, no. 12 (2002): 741–760.
[9] Emmons, Robert A., and Michael E. McCullough. "Counting Blessings Versus Burdens: An Experimental Investigation of Gratitude and Subjective Well-being in Daily Life." *Journal of Personality and Social Psychology* 84, no. 2 (2003): 377–389
[10] Amber. "An Interview with Dr. Stuart Brown, MD l Catalyst Ranch Blog-o-Rama." Blog. *Catalyst Ranch*, August 23, 2010.

http://blog.catalystranch.com/interviews/an-interview- with-dr-stuart-brown-md-co-author-of-play-how-it-shapes- the-brain-opens-the-imagination-and-invigorates-the-soul/.

Chapter 7
[1] Kenner, Robert. *Food, Inc*. Documentary, 2010.
http://www.takepart.com/foodinc.
[2] Koons, Deborah. *The Future of Food*. Documentary, http://www.thefutureoffood.com/.
[3] Brown, Lester. *Plan B 2.0 : Rescuing a Planet Under Stress and a Civilization in Trouble*. 1st ed. New York ;;London: W.W. Norton & Co., 2006. 164.
[4] Azeez, Gundula, and K. L. Hewlett. "The Comparative Energy Efficiency of Organic Farming", 2008. http://orgprints.org/12034/.
[5] Brown, Lester. *Plan B 2.0 : Rescuing a Planet Under Stress and a Civilization in Trouble*. 1st ed. New York ;;London: W.W. Norton & Co., 2006. 170-171.
[6] "Carbohydrates: Good Carbs Guide the Way - What Should I Eat? - The Nutrition Source - Harvard School of Public Health." Educational Institution. *Harvard School of Public Health*, n.d. http://www.hsph.harvard.edu/nutritionsource/what-should-you-eat/carbohydrates-full-story/.
[7] "Carbohydrates: Good Carbs Guide the Way - What Should I Eat? - The Nutrition Source - Harvard School of Public Health." Educational Institution. *Harvard School of Public Health*, n.d. http://www.hsph.harvard.edu/nutritionsource/what-should-you-eat/carbohydrates-full-story/.
[8] Cutler, Ellen. "Purification." *Boosting Immunity : Creating Wellness Naturally*. Len Saputo and Nancy Fass. Novato Calif.: New World Library, 2002. 82.
[9] Parker, Hilary. "Princeton University - A Sweet Problem: Princeton Researchers Find That High-fructose Corn Syrup Prompts Considerably More Weight Gain." Educational Institution. *Princton University*, April 22, 2010.
http://www.princeton.edu/main/news/archive/S26/91/22K07/.
[10] Hyman, Mark. "UltraWellness Lesson 2: Inflammation & Immune Balance." Health/Medical. *Drhyman.com*, April 28, 2010.
http://drhyman.com/blog/2010/04/28/ultrawellness-lesson-2-inflammation-immune-balance/.
[11] Berggren, Jason R., Matthew W. Hulver, and Joseph A. Houmard. "Fat as an Endocrine Organ: Influence of Exercise." *Journal of Applied Physiology* 99, no. 2 (2005): 757–764.
[12] Ornish, Dean. *Dr. Dean Ornish's Program for Reversing Heart Disease : the Only System Scientifically Proven to Reverse Heart Disease Without Drugs or Surgery*. 1st ed. New York: Random House, 1990.

[13] Lipton, Bruce. *The Biology of Belief : Unleashing the Power of Consciousness, Matter & Miracles*. Carlsbad Calif.: Hay House, 2008.

Chapter 8
[1] Cameron, James. *Avatar*. Action, Adventure, Fantasy, Sci-Fi, 2009.
[2] Oprah Radio. *Avoiding Every Day Toxins - Dr. Oz and Jane Houlihan of the Environmental Working Group.*, n.d.
[3] Darbre, P. D, A. Aljarrah, W. R Miller, N. G Coldham, M. J Sauer, and G. S Pope. "Concentrations of Parabens in Human Breast Tumors." *Journal of Applied Toxicology* 24, no. 1 (January 1, 2004): 5–13.
[4] Food and Drug Administration. "Selected Cosmetic Ingredients > Parabens." Government. *Food and Drug Administration*, n.d. http://www.fda.gov/cosmetics/productandingredientsafety/selectedcosmeticingredients/ucm128042.htm
[5] Environmental Protection Agency. "Volatile Organic Compounds | Indoor Air Quality | US EPA." Government. *Environmental Protection Agency*, n.d. http://www.epa.gov/iaq/voc.html.
[6] Gutierrez, David. "Antibacterial Soap Ingredient Triclosan May Be Harmful to Humans." Online News. *Natural News*, April 15, 2007. http://www.naturalnews.com/021703.html.
[7] Martin, Andrew. "Triclosan, an Antibacterial Chemical, Raises Safety Issues - NYTimes.com." Newspaper. *New York Times*, August 19, 2011. http://www.nytimes.com/2011/08/20/business/triclosan-an-antibacterial-chemical-in-consumer-products-raises-safety-issues.html?pagewanted=all.
[8] Oprah Radio. *Avoiding Every Day Toxins - Dr. Oz and Jane Houlihan of the Environmental Working Group.*, n.d.
[9] Oprah Radio. *Avoiding Every Day Toxins - Dr. Oz and Jane Houlihan of the Environmental Working Group.*, n.d.
[10] "Heavy Metal Toxicity - Heavy Metals, Arsenic, Mercury - Life Extension Health Concern." *LifeExtension.com*, n.d. http://www.lef.org/protocols/health_concerns/heavy_metal_toxicity_01.htm.
[11] Brown, Lester. *Plan B 2.0 : Rescuing a Planet Under Stress and a Civilization in Trouble*. 1st ed. New York ;;London: W.W. Norton & Co., 2006. 100.
[12] Brown, Lester. *Plan B 2.0 : Rescuing a Planet Under Stress and a Civilization in Trouble*. 1st ed. New York ;;London: W.W. Norton & Co., 2006. 106.
[13] Brown, Lester. *Plan B 2.0 : Rescuing a Planet Under Stress and a Civilization in Trouble*. 1st ed. New York ;;London: W.W. Norton & Co., 2006. 106.

Chapter 9

[1] Fabel, Klaus, and Gerd Kempermann. "Physical Activity and the Regulation of Neurogenesis in the Adult and Aging Brain." *NeuroMolecular Medicine* 10, no. 2 (February 20, 2008): 59–66.

[2] Shanor, Karen and Putnam, Frank. "States of Consciousness from Infancy to Nirvana". *The Emerging Mind*. Karen Shanor. 1st ed. Los Angeles: Renaissance Books, 1999. 57-60.

[3] Schwab, Deborah, Dana Davies, Tracy Bodtker, Lucy Anaya, Keren Johnson, and Maria Chaves. "A Study of Efficacy and Cost-effectiveness of Guided Imagery as a Portable, Self-administered, Presurgical Intervention Delivered by a Health Plan." *Advances in Mind-Body Medicine* 22, no. 1 (2007): 8–14.

[4] "Qigong." Non profit organization. *American Cancer Society*, November 1, 2008. http://www.cancer.org/Treatment/TreatmentsandSideEffects/ComplementaryandAlternativeMedicine/MindBodyandSpirit/qigong.

[5] Anderson, John W., Larry Trivieri, and Burton Goldberg. *Alternative Medicine: The Definitive Guide*. 2nd Updated. Celestial Arts, 2002.

[6] Weil, Andrew M.D. *Health and Healing*. New York, New York: Houghton Mifflin Company, 1995. 56.

[7] Ruiz, don Miguel. *The Four Agreements: A Practical Guide to Personal Freedom (Four-color Illustrated Ed.)*. 15 Anv. Amber-Allen Publishing, 2011.

[8] Carril-Grumberg, Ana. *Mind, Genes, Neuroplasticity and Enlightenment W/ Rudolph Tanzi, Ph.D Part 1*. Youtube channel, 2011. http://www.youtube.com/user/DeepakChopraGlobal#p/search/16/D0m4ruupgZs.

Chapter 10

[1] Little, Miles, Kim Paul, Christopher F. C Jordens, and Emma-Jane Sayers. "Survivorship and Discourses of Identity." *Psycho-Oncology* 11, no. 2 (March 1, 2002): 170–178.

[2] Little, Miles, Kim Paul, Christopher F. C Jordens, and Emma-Jane Sayers. "Survivorship and Discourses of Identity." *Psycho-Oncology* 11, no. 2 (March 1, 2002): 170–178.

[3] Benson, Herbert. *Timeless Healing : the Power and Biology of Belief*. New York NY: Scribner, 1996.

[4] Benson, Herbert. *Timeless Healing : the Power and Biology of Belief*. New York NY: Scribner, 1996.

[5] "NIMH · Statistics · Any Anxiety Disorder Among Adults." Government. *National Institute of Mental Health*, n.d. http://www.nimh.nih.gov/statistics/1ANYANX_ADULT.shtml.

[6] "Number of U.S. Kids on ADHD Meds Keeps Rising." *MedicineNet*, n.d. http://www.medicinenet.com/script/main/art.asp?articlekey=149916.

Chapter 11
[1] Emmons, Robert A. *Thanks!: How Practicing Gratitude Can Make You Happier*. Houghton Mifflin Harcourt, 2008.5.
[2] Abraham, Esther. *Ask and It Is Given : Learning to Manifest Your Desires*. Carlsbad Calif.: Hay House, 2004.141.
[3] Emmons, Robert A. *Thanks!: How Practicing Gratitude Can Make You Happier*. Houghton Mifflin Harcourt, 2008.4.
[4] Shanor, Karen and Spencer, John. "Mind-Body Medicine." *The Emerging Mind*. Karen Shanor. 1st ed. Los Angeles: Renaissance Books, 1999. 155-156.
[5] Pert, Candace. "The Chemical Communicators". *Healing and the Mind*. Bill Moyers. New York:Main Street Books, 1995. 177-193.
[6] Watkins, Philip C., Kathrane Woodward, Tamara Stone, and Russell L. Kolts. "GRATITUDE AND HAPPINESS: DEVELOPMENT OF A MEASURE OF GRATITUDE, AND RELATIONSHIPS WITH SUBJECTIVE WELL-BEING." *Social Behavior and Personality: An International Journal* 31, no. 5 (2003): 431–451.
[7] Collinge, William Ph.D. "Mind/Body Medicine & Cancer." *Collinge.org*, n.d. http://collinge.org/Hype.htm.
[8] Spiegel, David, HelenaC. Kraemer, JoanR. Bloom, and Ellen Gottheil. "EFFECT OF PSYCHOSOCIAL TREATMENT ON SURVIVAL OF PATIENTS WITH METASTATIC BREAST CANCER." *The Lancet* 334, no. 8668 (October 14, 1989): 888–891.

Chapter 12
[1] Benson, Herbert, and Miriam Z. Klipper. *The Relaxation Response*. HarperCollins, 2000.
[2] Mentgen, Janet. *Healing Touch*. Lakewood Colo.: Healing Touch, 1994.
[3] Goldstein, Joseph. *Insight Meditation : the Practice of Freedom*. 1st ed. Boston ;;London ;[New York N.Y.]: Shambhala ;;Distributed in the U.S. by Random House, 1993.
[4] University of Massachusetts Medical Center/Worcester., and Jon Kabat-Zinn. *Full Catastrophe Living : Using the Wisdom of Your Body and Mind to Face Stress, Pain, and Illness*. New York N.Y.: Delacorte Press, 1990.
[5] Wikipedia contributors. "Delta Wave." *Wikipedia, the Free Encyclopedia*. Wikimedia Foundation, Inc., September 5, 2012. http://en.wikipedia.org/w/index.php?title=Delta_wave&oldid=49155643 5.
[6] Deschenes, Cynthia L., and Susan M. McCurry. "Current Treatments for Sleep Disturbances in Individuals With Dementia." *Current Psychiatry Reports* 11, no. 1 (February 2009): 20–26.
[7] Lagopoulos, Jim, Jian Xu, Inge Rasmussen, Alexandra Vik, Gin S Malhi, Carl

F Eliassen, Ingrid E Arntsen, et al. "Increased Theta and Alpha EEG Activity During Nondirective Meditation." *Journal of Alternative and Complementary Medicine (New York, N.Y.)* 15, no. 11 (November 2009): 1187–1192.

Chapter 13
[1] Benson, Herbert, and Miriam Z. Klipper. *The Relaxation Response*. HarperCollins, 2000.
[2] Rossman, M.D. Martin L. *Guided Imagery for Self-Healing*. 2nd ed. HJ Kramer/New World Library, 2000.
[3] Hypnosis Motivation Institute. *Foundations in Hypnotherapy*. Online Distance Education. Foundations in Hypnotherapy, n.d.
[4] Hypnosis Motivation Institute. *Foundations in Hypnotherapy*. Online Distance Education. Foundations in Hypnotherapy, n.d.
[5] Hypnosis Motivation Institute. *Foundations in Hypnotherapy*. Online Distance Education. Foundations in Hypnotherapy, n.d.
[6] Shanor, Karen and Spencer, John. "Mind-Body Medicine." *The Emerging Mind*. Karen Shanor. 1st ed. Los Angeles: Renaissance Books, 1999. 155-156.
[7] Benson, Herbert, and Marg Stark. *Timeless Healing*. Softcover Ed. Scribner, 1997.
[8] Castaneda, Carlos. *Journey to Ixtlan: The Lessons of Don Juan*. Washington Square Press, 1991.

Chapter 14
[1] Myss, Caroline. *Invisible Acts of Power: Channeling Grace in Your Everyday Life*. Free Press, 2005. 18.
[2] *Jill Bolte Taylor's Stroke of Insight | Video on TED.com*, n.d. http://www.ted.com/talks/jill_bolte_taylor_s_powerful_stroke_of_insight.html.

Chapter 15
[1] Galewitz, Phil. "Healing Touch: A New Patient Outreach Program.", November 4, 2007. http://www.usatoday.com/news/health/2007-11-04-healing-touch_N.htm.
[2] Hansen, Bente. *The New World of Self-Healing: Awakening the Chakras & Rejuvenating Your Energy Field*. Llewellyn Publications, 2006.
[3] Mercier, Patricia. *The Chakra Bible: The Definitive Guide to Chakra Energy*. Sterling, 2007.
[4] De-stress, Stress Survey, Well-being, Stress Solutions, Lower Stress, Stress Management Tools, Institute of HeartMath." *Institute of HeartMath*, n.d. http://www.heartmath.org/.

www.ingramcontent.com/pod-product-compliance
Lightning Source LLC
LaVergne TN
LVHW041616070426
835507LV00008B/265